STORIES FROM SADDLE MOUNTAIN

AMERICAN INDIAN LIVES

SERIES EDITORS

Kimberly Blaeser
*University of Wisconsin, Milwaukee*

Brenda J. Child
*University of Minnesota*

R. David Edmunds
*University of Texas at Dallas*

K. Tsianina Lomawaima
*Arizona State University*

# Stories from Saddle Mountain

## Autobiographies of a Kiowa Family

HENRIETTA TONGKEAMHA
AND RAYMOND TONGKEAMHA

Edited by Benjamin R. Kracht
With Lisa LaBrada

UNIVERSITY OF NEBRASKA PRESS   Lincoln

Library of Congress Cataloging-in-Publication Data
Names: Tongkeamha, Henrietta, 1912–1993, author. |
Tongkeamha, Raymond, 1942– author. | Kracht, Benjamin
R., 1955– editor. | LaBrada, Lisa, contributor.
Title: Stories from Saddle Mountain : autobiographies of a Kiowa
family / Henrietta Tongkeamha and Raymond Tongkeamha ;
edited by Benjamin R. Kracht ; with Lisa LaBrada.
Description: Lincoln : University of Nebraska Press, [2021] | Series:
American Indian lives | Includes bibliographical references and index.
Identifiers: LCCN 2021001172
ISBN 9781496228116 (hardback)
ISBN 9781496228789 (epub)
ISBN 9781496228796 (pdf)
Subjects: LCSH: Kiowa Indians—Biography. | Tongkeamha,
Henrietta, 1912– | Tongkeamha, Raymond, 1942– | Kiowa
Indians—Oklahoma—Social life and customs—20th century. |
Saddle Mountain Region (Okla.)—Biography. | BISAC: SOCIAL
SCIENCE / Ethnic Studies / American / Native American
Studies | HISTORY / Indigenous Peoples of the Americas
Classification: LCC E99.K5 T664 2021 | DDC 978.004/97492—dc23
LC record available at https://lccn.loc.gov/2021001172

Set in Charis by Laura Buis.
Designed by N. Putens.

Dedicated to the Tongkeamha family
For my children, Robert and Elena

# CONTENTS

# ILLUSTRATIONS

# ACKNOWLEDGMENTS

Late one Sunday morning in early February 2020, southwestern Oklahoma temperatures soared in the eighties as Raymond Tongkeamha and I sat inside Cache Creek United Methodist Church—ten miles southeast of Carnegie—waiting for the service to begin. Almost ten years had passed since I last attended this rural Kiowa church for the funeral of my friend Dorothy Tsatoke Gray, and I was pleased to see that her son Cecil continued to hold services in her church. This day was especially joyous because everyone was gathering to celebrate the eighty-ninth birthday of renowned artist Chester Horse. Before the service began Raymond introduced me to Chester and informed him that we planned to publish an autobiography about the Tongkeamha family. Without hesitation Chester told Raymond, "Tell him everything!" As I reflect on Chester's encouraging words, I see that this project has been an enjoyable experience since its inception.

I am grateful to Lisa LaBrada for making her mother's memoirs available and to Raymond Tongkeamha for sharing his personal writings; their overwhelming support helped bring this project to fruition. Ethnographic fieldwork in May 2018 was funded by a Phillips Fund grant. Thanks go to Linda Musumeci, director of grants and fellowships at the American Philosophical Society, and to Daniel Swan and Christina Burke. As always, Henrietta Nelson at Holiday Inn Express ensured my stays in Lawton were comfortable. Claudia Lewis and Mary Joyce Swanda, director of the Apache Historical Society, and Tommie Riley, director of the Kiowa County Historical Society, kindly shared information and photographs of local landmarks.

xi

Christine Hallman, from the Department of Geography and Political Science at Northeastern State University, generously made map 1, for which I am thankful. Arnold Krupat and Alice Kehoe graciously provided critiques to strengthen the manuscript. I appreciate their helpful comments and constructive criticisms. Finally, special thanks go to Matthew Bokovoy and Heather Stauffer at the University of Nebraska Press for making this a pleasurable experience.

# INTRODUCTION

Kiowas have lived near mountains for time immemorial. Today at least half of the thirteen thousand enrolled members of the Kiowa Tribe of Oklahoma live north of the Wichita Mountains in the southwestern part of the state. Saddle Mountain, the northeastern sentinel of the Wichitas, is important to many Kiowa families, including the Tongkeamhas, who are spiritually connected to the surrounding countryside and have deep-rooted ties to a mission church about a mile north of the mountain. According to Raymond Tongkeamha, "You know, I don't think or know if there's any other place on earth that is more sacred or important to me than Saddle Mountain Kiowa Indian Baptist Church. And/or thirteen and a half miles south of Carnegie, Oklahoma. 'Tongkeamha Place.' It, Saddle Mountain, is 'sacred ground' to me."[1] Several years ago Raymond decided to share stories about life in these sacred grounds and began writing his life story. Around the same time his sister produced a copy of their mother's memoirs, written almost a half century earlier. Together their autobiographies—presented forthwith—relate stories about twentieth-century life in the Saddle Mountain countryside.

To appreciate the terrain around Saddle Mountain, I suggest driving fourteen miles northwest of Meers Store on State Highway 115, a zigzagging two-lane highway running between the red-hued Wichitas to the southwest and the limestone ridges of the Slick Hills to the northeast.[2] During the Middle Cambrian period, subterranean hot lava forced to the surface formed a dark gray-to-black gabbro, an igneous rock formation that solidified and uplifted several thousand feet. Sometime afterward a second hot granitic lava uplifted into the gabbro, forming the red granite that distinguishes the Wichitas today. Once the lava cooled, the surrounding land sank and filled with seawater, which over millions of years created the Slick Hills, a sediment of limestone over sandstone. Granite rock outcroppings in the mountains are visible through copses of post oak, blackjack oak, and eastern red cedar that grow in the gabbro layer.[3] North from Saddle Mountain the prairie opens up between Saddle Mountain and Pecan Creeks, which originate in the Slick Hills and meander northward toward the Washita River. Cottonwood, pecan, cedar, blackjack oak, elm, hackberry, walnut, mesquite, and chinaberry trees line the watercourses. Extending northwest are the solitary limestone tumuli of Longhorn Mountain, Unap Mountain, and Rainy Mountain. To the northeast Bally Mountain and Zodletone Mountain represent the northernmost extension of the Slick Hills. Deer, elk, rabbits, coyotes, bobcats, and feral hogs populate the countryside, while quail, owls, scissortail flycatchers, eagles, hawks, buzzards, and other fowl soar above. During warm spring afternoons one might espy a bull snake or rattlesnake slithering across the road.

In the late seventeenth century, Kiowas migrated southeast from the Bitterroot Mountains in Montana to the plains in search of a new equestrian lifestyle. Toward the end of the next century, they reached the Black Hills, where Lakotas and Cheyennes pushed them farther south to the Southwestern Plains (see Ortman and McNeil 2017, 9–10). Since then the Wichita Mountains and Slick Hills have been prominent features of ancestral Kiowa homelands. Upon conclusion of the Red River, or Southern Plains, War in May 1875, the Kiowas and their Comanche and Plains Apache allies were confined to the 2.8 million acre KCA Reservation in present-day southwestern Oklahoma (Kracht 2017, 35–39).[4] By the summer of 1882, the Kiowas established ten distinct communities north of the Wichita Mountains near favored geographic locations, including Saddle Mountain, whose inhabitants settled near the numerous springs emanating from underground wells in the region between the mountains and the hills (Kracht 2017, 25–26; 2018, 9).[5] By the end of the nineteenth

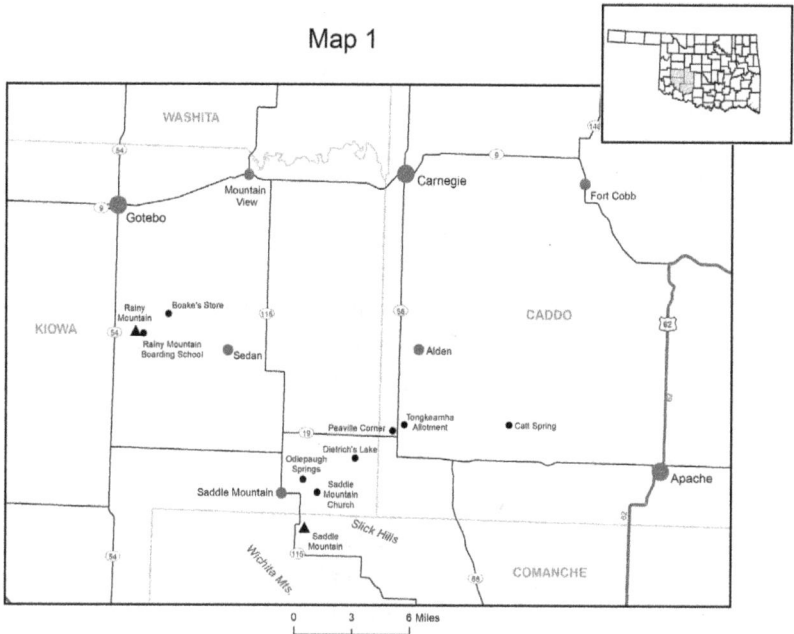

Map 1

1. Map of Saddle Mountain and vicinity. Courtesy of Christine Hallman, Department of Geography and Political Science, Northeastern State University.

century, every Kiowa received a 160-acre allotment, according to the provisions of the October 1892 Jerome Agreement that opened reservation lands for homesteading. Kiowa families led by Lucius Aitson, Domot, Odlepaugh, Spotted Horse, Kokom, Tonemah, Longhorn, and others chose their parcels near Saddle Mountain. After the August 1, 1901, "Opening," non-Indian homesteaders settling in the Saddle Mountain area engaged in agriculture and commerce. Neighboring communities sprang up: Boone, Alden, Hatchetville, and Broxton to the northeast; Cooperton to the west; and Sedan to the northwest. Larger towns appeared: Lawton—the largest—thirty-eight miles southeast; Apache, twenty-three miles east; Gotebo, twenty-three miles northwest; Mountain View, seventeen miles north; Carnegie, twenty-two miles north; Fort Cobb, thirty-one miles northeast; and Anadarko, forty-two miles northeast.

Today the Saddle Mountain countryside is largely bereft of Kiowas, except for a handful who stayed—or returned—home in the decades following World War II, when kinfolk moved closer to the small towns or migrated to near and distant cities. Reaching the homes of the remaining families often requires pulling off the highway and negotiating miles of dusty, gravel roads. Barns, sheds, silos, farm buildings, and ranch houses dotting the landscape signify non-Indian denizens, many descended from the original homesteaders. Farmers and ranchers grow wheat, soybeans, peanuts, pecans, hay, and cotton and raise livestock on lands they own or lease from Indians who still own allotments. The sparsely populated countryside makes it difficult to imagine that a community thrived there a hundred years ago. Raymond muses, "I know a lot of things took place there and a lot of people came and went. Baseball games, powwows, Fourth of July blowouts, church revivals, etc. Other tribes came. So many things, but today you couldn't imagine. All's quiet now and I'm sure their long ago presence still lingers. I think all the animals and birds today could tell you a lot of stories handed down from their great or great-great-grandparents."[6]

The Tongkeamhas have lived in the countryside around Saddle Mountain dating back to the original allotments chosen by their forebearers. Born near Gotebo, Henrietta Apayyat (1912–93) lived intermittently with her paternal grandparents, Oyebi (a.k.a. Apayyat or Albert Catt, 1874–1942) and Susie Tenegooah (1874–1920), at Catt Spring and her maternal grandparents, Odlepaugh "Buffalo Bird" (1853–1923) and Kol-an-on-da-mah "Buffalo Hoof Print" (1859–1934), near Saddle Mountain. In 1928 she married Weiser Tongkeamha (1912–91).[7] The newlywed couple moved thirteen and a half miles south of Carnegie to live with Weiser's parents, Kiowa Jim (d. 1939) and Fannie Tap-po-mah (1879–1950). They occupied a five-room house along East Cache Creek, where they raised five sons and five daughters: Wallace (1930–91), Clifton (1932–93), Lavena (1936–2009), Melissa (1940–2016), Raymond (b. 1942), James (1944–94), Bruce (1947–75), Becky (1949–95), Prenella (b. 1951), and Lisa (b. 1958).

2. Weiser and Henrietta Tongkeamha, circa 1928. Tongkeamha family photograph.

My first encounters with the Tongkeamhas occurred in April 1983, when I was a first-year doctoral student at Southern Methodist University. That semester I was Thomas M. Johnson's teaching assistant for cultural anthropology. One day after class Betty Tanedoah (b. 1931)—an older-than-average student—asked us if her husband could give a talk about Kiowa culture. Tom readily agreed because he had mentored my research on American Indian health care in Dallas and understood I needed to establish contacts in the urban Indian community. Memories of my first encounter with Clifton Tongkeamha evoke images of a six-foot-tall Native man resplendent in beaded buckskin and bone breastplate, donning an eagle-feather war bonnet and wielding an ornately beaded lance with two pendant eagle feathers. Years later Clifton claimed that the first words I uttered were "Oh, a lance!" Later that month Clifton and Betty invited me to attend an intertribal powwow at the National Guard Armory in Irving, Texas; during a pause between song sets, I was summoned to the emcee's table, where they gifted me a Pendleton blanket. In early May I met them at the Indian City dance grounds outside Anadarko to watch Clifton dance with the Black Leggings Warrior Society. Following a drum break, Clifton and Betty sponsored a giveaway, or "special," in which I was beckoned into the dance arena and presented with a Chief Joseph Pendleton blanket. Observing the pageantry associated with the dance, meeting some of Clifton and Betty's relatives, and being honored through ritual gift giving and incredible hospitality whet my curiosity to learn more about Kiowa culture and history. Though I was somewhat shy and intimidated by the reserved manner of some Kiowas, I found the experience exhilarating.

Several weeks passed before I summoned enough courage to call Clifton and Betty to thank them for introducing me to their culture. To my dismay Clifton gruffly answered the phone, but when I identified myself his voice softened, followed by, "What do you want from me?" (Clifton constantly grilled me with that question.) He related that he was sad and lonely because he and Betty had separated, so he invited me to his suburban home in Carrollton. My visits became more frequent when he began teaching me the Kiowa language. Not surprisingly, the first phrase he taught me was *tɔkoy kʼi emda*, "You're a white man." Clifton never minced words. Nevertheless, our friendship gradually developed over the next year. We met initially at Dallas area powwows and then traveled together to dances in Texas and Oklahoma. One evening, while visiting after a dance, Clifton remarked that he was taking me as a son because he was old enough to be my father. Moreover, he trusted me after deciding that I wasn't another two-faced photographer, teacher, or hobbyist seeking ethnographic details for personal gain. Clifton had been burned once when he was summoned to a grade school class to share a Kiowa story about Saynday, a legendary being. Unbeknownst to him, the teacher recorded his story, then published it as a children's book, listing him as merely a contributor. Such occurrences predisposed Clifton to subject me to "ethnographic tests."

During the Kiowa Gourd Clan ceremonial in July 1985, I visited Clifton and his family at the Tongkeamha encampment in Carnegie Park, where he introduced me to Henrietta and Weiser, some of his siblings, and other relatives, including Raymond. That afternoon Weiser escorted me throughout the encampment, introducing me to other families. In the ensuing years Clifton and I intermittently trekked to southwestern Oklahoma to attend dances and visit his parents. Upon initiating full-time fieldwork in early 1987, I often visited Henrietta and Weiser in their home several miles southeast of Carnegie.[8] I fondly recall visiting two years later, sitting between them on the living room couch. Simultaneously, Henrietta showed pictographic calendars made by her grandmother, while Weiser flashed old O-ho-mah Society photographs. It was difficult looking both ways at once. Over the next four years, I stopped by their home whenever I was in the area. Sadly, I remember visiting Weiser in 1991 a month before his passing, and with Henrietta two years later before her death.[9] Since then I've maintained a relationship with the family, though Raymond, Prenella, and Lisa are the sole survivors. Raymond and I reciprocally address each other as *tsegi*, "uncle," and I call Lisa and Prenella *tsayi*, "aunt."

While we were visiting under the family shade at Carnegie Park during the July 2016 Kiowa Gourd Clan festivities, Raymond told me about his mom's memoirs, which he had recently read.[10] My interest piqued when he described some details, though months passed before I saw the document. In early May 2017, following the Sunday postservice meal, Lisa and I sat at a table in the house trailer that until recently served as Saddle Mountain Church and cleared a space for her to place the spiral notebook. The top line of the opening page was "This is the Story of My Life." Eagerly scanning through the notebook, I read about a Peyote meeting, revivals, and Christmas encampments at Saddle Mountain Church; subsistence activities; trips to neighboring towns; rides in cars and trains; and boarding and public schools. Though much of the manuscript eulogizes her grandparents, Henrietta's stories provide a Kiowa woman's perspective of early twentieth-century life in southwestern Oklahoma.[11] Lisa describes her mother:

I'm Lisa Gay Tongkeamha LaBrada.

My mama had given me my Kiowa Indian name, Toyegadaye. The meaning meant "She Stands Away from Here," or "She Stands." Previously it had belonged to one of my grandmothers. My loving memory of my mama is to see her sitting in a chair either beadworking or at her Singer, push pedal sewing machine. I asked her one time how did she manage to clothe us all? She looked at me as though I asked her a silly question and make me feel small. But she always had a clear answer for me.

I loved hearing about the life she lived with her grandparents. My mama was a very strong Baptist Christian. I remember her asking me to get her Bible, she would help me find the place. I being very young at the age of seven. She would recite the "Lord's Prayer" by heart. I remember being so amazed even as young as I was! I wanted to be able to do the same.

The wonderful mornings I would wake up to the warm room. My daddy would already have the wood stove hot and the heat would be making the whole room warm. Mama would already have breakfast made and all the while they would both be talking Kiowa. She would come and get me up out of bed and take me to the wash stand to wash my face and hands with the warm water and soap. My place at the table was sitting on the right side of mama. My dad would begin praying in Kiowa.

I was the last of twelve children. I remember my brother James teaching me to tell time and my brother Bruce teaching me to tie my shoestrings.

I went almost everywhere with my parents. They knew so many people and had more relatives. My mama, I loved so much. She was such a beautiful lady. All she wore was lipstick and rouge on her pretty face, just a smidgen, and always had the longest hair. She kept her hair neatly rolled into a bun then kept into place with a hairnet and bobby pins. Her hair always smelled of "Three Flowers" and she wore glasses. Because of her high arch she always had to wear a ¾ inch heel. Mama was a lady that always wore her jewelry and a very pretty dress that went with the occasion.

Springtime in the country is wonderful. My mama would have me cleaned up after breakfast and she would be ready to sit down and sew her beadwork. Beaded belts was our choice of making money together. She taught me to beadwork the stringed loom on the frame then she did the attaching to the belt. We once sold a lot of our belts to the Mohawk Lodge in Clinton, OK. Financially helped mom out a lot. She beaded moccasins for my brother Clifton and many Kiowa traditional ornaments for our dancing regalia. She made all of my accessories as a young girl. Many, many, many shawls. Too many to count that we both made together. I did the fringing and she made a lot of the beautiful decorations of her own.

One day I asked mama, "Can we go to the playpark?" I think I was eight years old. She said, "Come sit beside me. I'm going to teach you how to embroider." That was to be my beginning to sew. To me my mama could sew anything. The house would be quiet until she began to sing. I loved to hear my mother sing. She would tell me which song belong to her aunts. There is a song her grandfather Odlepaugh made. There are many Kiowa songs made by different relatives. Great grandmother Ananthy [Kol-an-on-da-mah] also composed a beautiful Kiowa church hymn.

My mother had given my youngest son Carlos his Kiowa name. From then after, my son Carlos would also be known as Satanta White Bear. My eldest son James Daniel's Kiowa name is Goonuhoyl.

My mother Henrietta was an old fashion person, she would say. Very fluent in speaking Kiowa, I can still hear her voice. Never high pitch or a shrill her voice was. But just the right, light level and very clear with strength.

The year 1968 we finally moved to Carnegie, OK. My mom had many friends that she loved to sew with. She would drive to the church dining halls after picking up some other friends. I loved to see and hear her laugh.

Living in town made it a lot easier for both of my parents and I. It was better being [close] to the grocery store and the Carnegie school and the laundromat. I know in the beginning how my mom had to wash our clothes by hand. I know there were a lot of things and situations that were beginning to be hard on my mama when we lived in the country. Even though we didn't have an inside bathroom or a washer and dryer. I never heard my mother raise her voice about those issues.

I thank God for my mama having extra loving and caring grandparents Odlepaugh and Ananthy [Kol-an-on-da-mah]. They taught my mama Henrietta and her sister Margaret, their brother Bruce extremely well.

I also thank God that they still had a father, Fremont. He was there to love them.

As I sat beside my mama's hospital bed, she's in a coma. I told my mama I was so happy for her. She's going to be going home to see everyone, including her mother. I still remember holding her hand and half of my face laying on her warm chest. She squeezed my hand very slightly and I seen two tears drop on the left side of her cheek. I had my tissue and I softly dabbed her face. Mama went home.[12]

According to Lisa, Henrietta began penning her memoirs after she and Weiser moved to Carnegie in 1968. "My mom must have been really happy and satisfied. Moving into their new home, she wanted to settle down to do her writing."[13] Sometime before her passing Henrietta gave the notebook, some photographs, and other personal items to Lisa, probably because she was the youngest, lived nearby, and spent a lot of time with her parents. Lisa describes the day she received the "book."

The day my mama gave me her biography, I felt overwhelmed. I was chosen to get my mother's book. It happened on a Saturday afternoon in June. She was getting ready to go to the powwow at Red Buffalo Hall. She had me open her trunk of pretty shawls that she didn't want anyone getting their hands on. She got out a couple of her shawls and picked up the book of hers. I knew she'd write in it when she said she was alone in the house. At the moment, I kind of got shaky. She handed her book to me. I was overwhelmed! She chose me to take her book! She said, "You can keep it. I have been writing and writing in it telling my life and how I was cared for. Maybe my book means nothing. But I loved all of my family and my grandparents because they raised me. And Lisa, maybe someday it will be made into a real book for everyone to see how wonderful my grandparents were to me. They lived back then, and they lived the old way."[14]

Lisa has possessed the notebook—and associated materials—ever since, and Raymond was unaware of it until recently.[15]

After briefly examining the manuscript, we concurred that it contains enough valuable information to publish. Four months later Lisa and her husband, Carlos, graciously invited me into their home near Alden to photograph the eighty-eight-page notebook. Afterward, during a delicious lunch of NDN soup and fry bread, we discussed how to move the project forward.[16] Back home in Tulsa, I spent the next half year transcribing the manuscript. The following spring I stayed in Lawton for two weeks to conduct background research. First, Raymond, Lisa, Carlos, and I spent two long days proofreading my transcribed copy to verify its concordance with the notebook, which was photographed a second time for archiving.[17] For the duration of my stay, Raymond and I traversed back roads, where he enhanced my knowledge of the greater Saddle Mountain area, showing me the location of former homes, stores, schools, swimming holes, and the old Tongkeamha homestead. We photographed specific places mentioned by Henrietta, including Catt Spring, Rainy

Mountain School ruins, and the ghost town of Gotebo. Our search also led us to local historical societies for photographs and backstories about these locations. Raymond, Lisa, and I sorted through family photographs to complement her stories. Despite the addition of photographs, we knew the manuscript was too short for a book.

Serendipitous events make ethnographic fieldwork rewarding. Several days before leaving Lawton, Raymond and I were visiting on his front porch when he showed me a notebook in which he had been writing his memoirs the past two years. After reading some of his stories about life on the Tongkeamha allotment and the larger Saddle Mountain community, I recognized the value of his memoirs and asked to publish them alongside his mom's. He readily agreed but said that his life story was unfinished. True to his word, he continued writing and submitted additional notebook entries in June, November, and December 2019, completing his life story.[18] As with Henrietta's, his notebooks were photographed and transcribed, then mailed to him for proofreading. Additional corrections and edits were communicated through phone texts. Raymond's memoirs complement Henrietta's and carry the family narrative into the twenty-first century.

In the semiautobiographical *The Way to Rainy Mountain* (1969), N. Scott Momaday portrays Rainy Mountain as a "critical template" defining "the heart of Kiowa country" (Teuton 2010, 55). Though encampments near Rainy Mountain constitute one of the early Kiowa settlements on the reservation, the surrounding countryside remains largely uninhabited today, evident by the ruins of the abandoned boarding school along its eastern base (Kracht 2017, 25–26). Nevertheless, Momaday (1976, 61) chose this solitary limestone knoll to symbolize Kiowa homelands despite spending his childhood on the Navajo and Jemez reservations, where his parents taught at Indian schools. Returning to southwestern Oklahoma years later to attend his grandmother's funeral, he perceived the rugged landscape as isolated and lonely until personal experiences, stories, and histories allowed him to understand his ancestors' attachment to the land

(Teuton 2010, 62). Conversely, Henrietta always lived near Saddle Mountain, and, despite military service and jobs elsewhere, Raymond never stayed away very long. Personal memories and family stories have connected them to the Saddle Mountain community for over a century. As noted by Lisbeth Haas (2011, 32), Native histories are "encoded in physical space" and describe a "social geography of indigenous places." For the Tongkeamhas that place is Saddle Mountain.

STORIES FROM SADDLE MOUNTAIN

# 1 Henrietta Tongkeamha's Memoirs

## Overview

According to Bureau of Indian Affairs (BIA) records, Fremont Apa-yyat and Lula Kau-quo-ye's oldest daughter, Henrietta, was born on May 18, 1912, near Gotebo. Fremont was Susie Tenegooah and Albert Catt's oldest son, and Lula was Kol-an-on-da-mah and Odle-paugh's third daughter. Following the death of her mother in 1918, Henrietta intermittently lived with both sets of grandparents over the next ten years. Like other turn-of-the-century allottees, they had selected their 160-acre parcels near creeks for access to water and timber (Lynn-Sherow 2004, 133). Albert and Susie settled on her allotment just northeast of the Slick Hills at Catt Spring, fed by an underground well that provided an ample supply of water. Today water piped from its depths is sold to a bottling company. Renowned for the spring emanating from a subterranean source in the Slick Hills, the Odlepaughs lived on Kol-an-on-da-mah's allotment two miles northwest of Saddle Mountain. Elderly Kiowas reminiscence about being baptized in the cool waters of Odlepaugh Springs (Hall 2000, 59; Kracht 2018, 245, fig. 10).

3. Catt Spring, May 2018. Photograph by Benjamin Kracht.

Odlepaugh and Kol-an-on-da-mah were born in the waning years of the horse and buffalo culture, whereas Albert and Susie Catt were born on the cusp of its collapse. Despite their age differences, they lived on the reservation before allotment and witnessed the transition from tipis, horses, buffalo hunts, warfare, raiding, trading, vision quests, and Sun Dances to houses, homesteaders, towns, stores, trains, cars, and new religions. The former equestrians pursuing migratory bison herds had become sedentary and dependent on government commodities, though rations ended in 1901 because the BIA expected them to become subsistence farmers. However, Kiowas had never been farmers, so allotments were not chosen based on the BIA's notion of row-crop farming; inexperience was not conducive to becoming successful commercial farmers (Lynn-Sherow 2004, 131, 135). After homesteading, indigenous subsistence patterns shifted toward a "mixed economy of stock raising, wild food gathering, domestic agricultural production, cash from leasing and annuities, government rations, and wage labor." But within a couple of years, many began leasing to non-Indian farmers, and by 1909 at least 70 percent of Kiowa lands were leased (131, 135, 137, 140). Compared to other Kiowas, the Oyebis and Odlepaughs fared relatively well. Both had gardens, horses, and barns; raised cattle and chickens; and maintained orchards. Besides leasing some of their lands, they helped white neighbors harvest wheat and butcher animals. Wage labor added to the household income. Elderly Kiowas from that era recall miscellaneous farmwork, such as baling hay, picking cotton, or harvesting peanuts or wheat, sometime in their life. Until recently, numerous Native men could be seen early in the morning congregating at the "employment agency"—southeast corner of Main and Carnegie—in Carnegie, waiting for local ranchers to hire day laborers. Years ago Raymond went there and was hired by a rancher, though the type of work wasn't specified. He cowboyed that day, rounding up calves and loading them on trailers. Having recently returned from living in Dallas, he hadn't ridden horses for a long time and was sore for a week.[1]

Before the reservation was opened for homesteading, roads and trails connected military posts with government offices. Afterward horse-drawn wagons, hacks, and eventually cars traversed dirt roads linking the communities and towns established by settlers. Transition from a subsistence to a cash economy often necessitated daylong or overnight trips to Lawton and Anadarko for business or supplies, or shorter trips to small towns or country stores that sold groceries, drugs, and dry goods. Old buildings in Apache— founded in 1901—include the former drug stores on the northwest and southeast corners of Coblake Street and Evans Avenue as well as Warner's Grocery, which is now a school supply store. Saddle Mountain Store opened on January 2, 1902, as a general store, fourth-class post office, blacksmith shop, barbershop, and Model T garage. Weekend baseball games were played in a field behind the store, which closed on May 31, 1955. Today the cobblestone store added in 1907 survives. In 1900 the Chicago, Rock Island and Pacific

4. Raymond Tongkeamha in front of the old Warner's Grocery, Apache, Oklahoma, May 2018. Photograph by Benjamin Kracht.

Railroad company laid a rail line from Chickasha ninety-eight miles west to Magnum. Lines connecting Anadarko and Lawton were constructed the following year (Bell, Buzbee, and Riffel 2001, 28). The next year Gotebo was established near the Rock Island depot, approximately seven miles northwest of Rainy Mountain. During its heyday Gotebo was a thriving town, boasting two schools, eight churches, an oil refinery, a brick factory, four cotton gins, three banks, three dry goods stores, four produce houses, four grocery stores, and two meat markets. The latter were butcher shops where Indians came to buy *bote*, or tripe, which is served like the Mexican dish *menudo* (see Palmer 2003, 81–82). Weiser Tongkeamha used to joke that he was going to "bote-e-go."[2] Other businesses included four produce houses, two lumberyards, two hardware stores, two furniture stores, nine garage/filling stations, four oil distributers, two hotels, four barbershops, two tailor shops, and several cafés.[3]

Regarding early twentieth-century race relations, Henrietta's grandparents seemed to have positive relationships with white neighbors, though some town merchants were unpopular because they charged Indians higher prices for having credit accounts; discrimination was rampant in towns whose inhabitants were predominately non-Indian. African Americans who settled in Oklahoma Territory, however, were subjected to racial violence. Before 1907 public hangings in the Oklahoma territories represented "western frontier justice," but after statehood lynching emerged as a form of racial control associated with Jim Crow segregation introduced by immigrants from southern states. Although African Americans moving to Oklahoma perceived it as "a destination of hope, where they could prosper without the laws in southern states that codified racism and repression, what was to be a promised land proved to be a great disillusionment." Such was the case for Bennie Simmons, who was lynched in Anadarko on June 13, 1913. Undoubtedly driven by the postbellum image of Black men lusting for white women, Bennie was accused of murdering sixteen-year-old Susie Church. A lynch mob wrested Simmons from armed guards, dowsed him with coal oil, set him on fire, and hanged him from the limb of a cottonwood tree. According to a newspaper account, he "prayed and shrieked in agony as the flames reached his flesh, but his cries were drowned out by yells and jeers from the crowd." As Simmons lost consciousness, the mob fired volleys into his body. No one was ever prosecuted, even though the perpetrators did not disguise themselves (Allen et al. 2000, 166, 179). (Many undoubtedly became members of the Anadarko klavern that formed in 1924.)[4] Evan Woodson (2015, viii, xv, 38–40, 50–58, 61) notes that lynchings in Oklahoma peaked during the 1910s. African Americans living south of an imaginary line extending southwest from Miami to Altus were prone to racially motivated, southern-style violence; Anadarko is barely south of the line crisscrossing the state. Between 1910 and 1928 twenty-eight Blacks were lynched in Oklahoma. Lynchings became a tool of state making.

Indians undoubtedly witnessed the lynching; Kol-an-on-da-mah recorded the event in a calendar she kept in a notebook. As in other

Plains tribes—Lakotas, Blackfoots, Mandans, Hidatsas, Cheyennes, and Plains Apaches—calendar-keeping traditions are maintained in several Kiowa families. James Mooney's *Calendar History of the Kiowa Indians* (1898) is based on the Little Bluff, Little Bear, and Anko calendars, and a calendar made by Silver Horn was discovered recently. Among Plains tribes, calendars were pictographs on buffalo robes depicting "winter counts" as notable events that happened that year; Kiowa calendars differed by adding "summer counts." Calendar keepers knew the stories represented by each picture (see Greene 2009, 1–9). George Hunt (1881–1942), or Set-maun-tee, "Bear Paw," took one of Kol-an-on-da-mah's calendars and never returned it. Hunt spent part of his youth at Fort Sill, where his uncle Tah-bone-mah (a.k.a. I-See-O) was an army scout for Indian Troop L. Hunt played with other children at the post, where he learned English. Fluent in Kiowa, English, and Plains sign language, Hunt interpreted for Mooney and scholars of Kiowa history, including Hugh L. Scott, Wilbur S. Nye, and Alice Marriott. Hunt also interpreted for the 1935 Santa Fe Laboratory of Anthropology field expedition (Kracht 2017, xv). The George Hunt calendar that appears in *The Ten Grandmothers* (Marriott 1945, 292–305) could be Kol-an-on-da-mah's first calendar. Henrietta showed me the second one in 1989. I never saw it again.

Public schools materialized on the former KCA Reservation in the wake of the opening. Following statehood, the Oklahoma legislature mandated that children ages eight to sixteen enroll in public schools (Bell, Buzbee, and Riffel 2001, 125). By then Kiowa children attended district schools—mostly rural, one-room schoolhouses—alongside non-Indians. Francis Prucha (1984, 823n) observes that by 1912, nearly one-half of American Indian students were enrolled in public schools versus government and mission schools. Henrietta attended public and boarding schools through the eighth grade. Her aunt and uncles attended Mountain Home School, located over a mile west from their home at Catt Spring. Opened in 1909, the one-room schoolhouse situated next to a knoll in the Slick Hills closed in the late 1930s.

Henrietta was seven years old when she attended Rainy Mountain Boarding School during its last months of operation. Founded in September 1893 for Kiowa families living in the western districts of the reservation, the campus buildings were arrayed along the eastern base of the limestone ridge immortalized by N. Scott Momaday. Despite proximity to Rainy Mountain Creek, the school faced chronic water shortages and poor sanitation and was constantly plagued by outbreaks of trachoma and other diseases, forcing it to close in June 1920 (Ellis 1996, 164–68, 178–94). Henrietta's silence regarding the school's deplorable conditions is puzzling. Instead, she mentions trips to Gotebo and the nearby Indian trading post owned by Corwin Boake. Located one mile east of the campus, Kiowas called Boake's Store Tokio "long building" because of its 125-foot length. Parents and grandparents camped nearby when they came to visit students. Henrietta left Rainy Mountain School twenty-seven days before its official closing. Shortly after the school ceased operations, the Indian trade dwindled, forcing the store to close in 1935. Indians sold their allotments and moved elsewhere, and Gotebo rapidly declined. Barely visible from the road today, ruins of the boys' dormitory are the sole clue that the school existed; Tokio's walls remain intact, though the roof collapsed long ago; long-abandoned buildings along Commercial Avenue attest that Gotebo once was a bustling town. After Rainy Mountain School, Henrietta attended Riverside Indian School, Fort Sill Indian School, and public schools in Sedan and Saddle Mountain. Most of her memories are of Riverside. Opened in Anadarko in 1871 and relocated north of the Washita River in 1878–79, Riverside is the oldest federal Indian boarding school. Henrietta details a regimented lifestyle involving identification numbers, daily routines, inspections, discipline, and corporal punishment. She reflects on her boarding school experiences without acrimony, analogous to Momaday's (1969, 10) grandmother, who "without bitterness" "bore a vision of deicide" following the collapse of the horse and buffalo culture.

Living with both sets of grandparents exposed Henrietta to the

5. Ruins of boys' dorm at the Rainy Mountain School, March 2007. Photograph by Benjamin Kracht.

differences between two religious traditions that first appeared on the KCA Reservation during the final decades of the nineteenth century—Peyotism and Christianity. After the Sun Dance was abandoned, prophet movements and the Ghost Dance failed to restore the horse and buffalo culture, so new religions, amalgamated with older traditions, filled the void, especially Peyotism, which aligns with indigenous beliefs and practices. As a medicine, peyote offers healing, and as a teacher, it embraces spiritual and ethical ways of living (Maroukis 2010, 59–60; Kracht 2018, 156, 224–27). Peyote or tipi meetings are held to celebrate birthdays and national holidays, heal the sick, offer gratitude for the convalesced, and bless departing soldiers and returning veterans. Sometime in 1918 Henrietta was taken into a meeting because she had a fever; she remembers the attendees, including Ned Brace and Belo Cozad (a.k.a. Billose or Below), who later served as interpreters and consultants for the 1935 Santa Fe Laboratory of Anthropology field school (Kracht 2017, 30). Notably,

6. Dixie Store and Davis Grocery Store, on Commercial Avenue, Gotebo, Oklahoma, May 2018. Photograph by Benjamin Kracht.

Smithsonian Institution ethnologist James Mooney attended a tipi meeting near Albert Catt's home in 1918 and suggested organizing and chartering as the Native American Church to shield Peyotists from prosecution if proposed anti-Peyote legislation was passed (LaBarre 1957, 31–32; Kracht 2018, 165). After the official church charter, the Oyebis sponsored a Peyote meeting the following year, when Henrietta's uncle returned from the military. After butchering a cow to feed at least a dozen guests, everybody enjoyed the delicacy *bote* (see Palmer 2003, 81–82).[5]

Kiowas converting to Christianity were attracted by the good works of the missionaries and field matrons who cared for the infirmed, buried their dead, and facilitated the transition from tipis to houses. Most important, perceiving Jesus as a guardian spirit and God as a new source of *dɔdɔ* "power" meshed well with indigenous beliefs in a power force permeating the universe, except God's power was available to everyone instead of a select few who had received power through visions. Although some resisted conversion, Christianity slowly spread from person to person, family to family, as former traditions were modified and melded with Christian beliefs. Like Peyotism, Christianity provides healing and promotes healthy living. Today many family histories feature stories of conversion (Kracht 2018, 156, 224–27). The Tongkeamhas remain steadfast Christians today.

Supported by the Women's Baptist Home Mission Society, thirty-one-year-old Isabel Crawford (1865–1961) arrived at the Elk Creek mission to work among the Kiowas in November 1893. On April 10, 1896, she moved farther southeast to the Saddle Mountain community with the goal of building a mission (Whiteley 2015, 8, 54, 68–69). Crawford initially camped with Kiowa families along Saddle Mountain Creek, which she describes as one of the "many soft-water springs that rise in the foot-hills of the Wichita Mountains." For the next ten years, Crawford lived among the Saddle Mountain Kiowas and established a mission society that raised money to build a chapel, dedicated on April 12, 1903. Odlepaugh and Kol-an-on-da-mah—her allotment abutted the western boundary of the mission tract—were among the sixty-four charter members in attendance (Crawford 1915, 16, 211–13, 222).

After enduring months of treatment with quinine for "acute phthisis" at age eighteen, Crawford lost most of her hearing, which compelled her to use a listening tube fastened to a necklace chain. Kiowas nicknamed her T'ɔkama, "No Ears," or "[Woman who is] hard of hearing." Overcoming her disability, Crawford—fluent in American Sign Language—quickly learned Plains sign language to communicate with her congregants. Kiowas in the Saddle Mountain area who converted to Christianity gave her another name, Gee-ah-ho-ah-go-ma, or "She gave us the Jesus way." Influenced by Crawford's teachings, some converts composed hymns sung a cappella in the Kiowa language that convey deep spiritual feelings and reflect family values and history (see Lassiter 2005). Crawford left the Saddle Mountain mission on December 3, 1906, though she returned several times in the late 1920s. Henrietta probably saw Crawford at the 1927, 1928, and 1929 Christmas encampments (Whiteley 2015, 27–28, 69–70, 99, 159, 162–63, 167; Kracht 2018, 58–59, 256). After leaving Saddle Mountain, Crawford wrote several books about her Kiowa mission work. Many Kiowa elders best remember *Joyful Journey: Highlights on the High Way* (1951). Earlier works include *From Tent to Chapel at Saddle Mountain* ([1909?]) and *Kiowa: The History of a Blanket Indian Mission* (1915). Crawford died on November 18, 1961, in Hamilton, Ontario, and her remains were sent to Oklahoma, where she was interred four days later at Saddle Mountain Cemetery. Revs. James Treat and Barry Shongo led the services.[6]

Life with the Odlepaughs centered around Saddle Mountain Church. Henrietta said, "When we were living at Saddle Mountain, the first thing that I noticed was my grandparents going to church. And that's when Isabel Crawford was already there."[7] Henrietta met Weiser Tongkeamha at Saddle Mountain Church in 1926, after his parents began attending. Formerly members of the Native American Church, Kiowa Jim and Fannie converted to Christianity when Peyote doctors failed to save their son Frank's life the previous year (Kracht 2018, 154, 178). Henrietta and Weiser were sixteen years old when they married on July 10, 1928. Vivian Tsatoke Komardly (1927–2018) once told Raymond that her parents, Rev. Cecil Hunting Horse (1891–1978) and Jennie Haumpy Horse (1892–1985), were the matchmakers who brought them together. Shortly before she passed away, Raymond asked her to repeat the story, but she could not remember it.[8]

Like other Kiowas who converted to Christianity, Odlepaugh and Kol-an-on-da-mah enjoyed dancing and feasting when relatives came to visit for several days to a week, which perturbed the Indian agents who expected their charges to stay home and farm their allotments. Henrietta mentions their "relics" and "costumes" from the past — War Dance regalia they wore at dances. Notwithstanding antidance policies of Indian agency officials and missionaries, Kiowas never lost their passion for dancing (see Kracht 2018, 119–45; 2012). Odlepaugh and Kol-an-on-da-mah took Henrietta to dances at Dietrich's Lake. Tom Dietrich, of Comanche-Anglo descent, owned an allotment eighteen miles south of Carnegie, where he connected a reservoir to Cache Creek. Situated in a valley of the Slick Hills, Dietrich's Lake was an ideal location for the intertribal dances Dietrich sponsored in the late 1910s (Kracht 2012, 296). A few years later dances moved west to another dance ground. In 1923 Frank Rush bought land north of Cache near the Wichita Mountains and developed Craterville Park, a tourist resort. Annual Indian dances and other festivities were conducted there every August until Rush's death in 1933. Afterward the annual dance moved to the county fairgrounds in Anadarko and became the American Indian Exposition, held every August. Besides dancing, Craterville and the exposition featured archery, horse races, and agricultural and handicraft exhibits. Odlepaugh and Kol-an-on-da-mah also danced on July Fourth at the Lone Bear dance grounds southeast of Carnegie. Dances there were discontinued after a tornado carried off a woman in 1928 (Kracht 2012, 296–99; 2017, 66). Like other converts, the Odlepaughs continued dancing and living in tent or tipi communities. Large crowds assembled for powwows or Christian events. Elderly Kiowas I interviewed in 1987 gleefully provided details about Christmas and revival encampments that oftentimes lasted over a week (Kracht 2018, 147, 153–54, 243–44). Henrietta believes that camping and dancing traditions are not incompatible with being Christian.

According to Gretchen Bataille and Kathleen Sands (1994, 188), Native women's autobiographies emphasize private lives, daily events and activities, and relationships with family members. Similarly, Henrietta's narrative memorializes her grandparents and reveals deep sorrow for the deaths of Grandma Susie and Grandpa Odlepaugh. Though she briefly mentions marriage and the birth of her children, her story ends with several tragedies: the tornado that destroyed the Odlepaugh homestead and the passing of Kol-an-on-da-mah; her brother, Bruce; and her father. Because her narrative abruptly ends in 1936, she doesn't mention Oyebi's death six years later, nor does she describe living conditions on the Tongkeamha allotment during the Great Depression. Fortunately, during our final interview session in 1993, Henrietta described life in the 1930s and 1940s.

My granddaughter asked me one day; she lives in Tulsa now with her husband. She said, "Grandma, were you all here during the Depression days?" And I said, "Sure, we were here. I was a young married woman then." And she said, "How did you all survive?" I said, "Well, somehow we did; we're all here. Me and Grandpa." I said, "Yes, we were here during the Depression days." I said, "We had to buy food with stamps; we were allowed to buy sometimes just one item. So much sugar. You were allowed to buy a pair of shoes that would have to last us long. No tires, no luxuries, nothing. We had to park our car because the tires were worn out, and we had no tires. So it was really hard; it was very hard. But one thing, my in-laws, he had cows, and my father-in-law, and then he raises garden, and that's where we get our food, like potatoes, all those things that you plant. Green beans, and I tell you it's really hard. We were just allowed so many pounds of sugar, and no more. Whatever you had, whatever you got, you had to make it last.

"All stores are the same. We had a book. They give us, they call them mills in change, I think. It wasn't real money. But it was worth so little, in change. In change of money, they give us, what's the name of it, mills, I can't think of the other. It's not money, but it's not a metal either. I think I had some for a long time. That's what they used to give us in change, you know. It's not worth much, but we can use it again, we could buy groceries or something in the line of food. And then we had books for stamps; we were allowed only for shoes. And we can buy shoes. Each person is allowed a pair of shoes. So some of us saved our shoes. That's the way it was, just like sometimes they say, from rags to riches. They talk about how they saved their shoes during the summer so they could have them during the winter. So that's the way some of us were. Yes, they sent to school barefooted. To save their shoes. It was really hard."[9]

The absence of electricity and indoor plumbing necessitated gathering kindling and fetching water. Laundry was an overwhelming task for Henrietta, having raised ten children before steam laundries opened in Carnegie.

You build a fire; put a big pot of warm, hot water in there; and then you have a stick. My mother-in-law washes that way, and I did for a while, until the laundries were open. She had a long stick that the old man make for her; he cleaned the barks, had it all cleaned. She would soak her whites in that; some of them do that. On a fire in a big pot. She'd rub them first; see, you rub our clothes first, and then you wring them and put them in the boiling container over the fire. And then stir it around, stir it around, and then, by the time, put a little of that lye, lye, in that water, and then after while take it out, put it in another tub, and start rubbing again. And those clothes come out very white and clean. And then you have two tubs of rinsing water; rinse them once, wring them with your hands, then rinse them the second time, then hang them up, then they're through. Dry, get them off, then you fold them, and then there was no starch. . . . And you keep the fire up to keep water hot. . . .

Of course, the man helps sometimes; they'll build the fire for you and get your water, change water, and get clear rinsing water. And then you stop for a lunch break; you go to the house. I did. I went to the house. I made lunch for my children, my family, and the girls, and some of the boys helped wash dishes too. James and my older boy that died [Clifton], he'd wash the dishes; they were the oldest. Wallace was the oldest. So they knew there was a lot of work. I'd go back down the creek; we lived near the creek, then I'd go on and finish the rest of the laundry. And by evening I'm through hanging them out, and sometimes it's so hot, it don't take long for the laundry to dry. You get them off and put the next basket up, hang them, next basket, the wet clothes to dry. And then next come ironing, so those things are just routine for women. Every so often, every week you do laundry. Sometimes I like to do it twice to keep it from piling up. So that was where the hard-working days.

This lady, my neighbor, she took her clothes to the laundry. She say, "You ought to let, this five boys and five girls to wash for." She say, "You make time to take your clothes to the laundry." She said, "It's a lot easier. A lot easier than the old way." She said, "I started taking mine." I didn't know how to use the machines. That's when they had the steam washers. You turn the handle through the wringer; they come through to the rinsing water and then to the next rinsing water. So that was better than wringing them out with your hands. You didn't have to wring. I didn't really care to go. I said, "Really, I don't know how to use those machines." So, she said, "I'll go with you." She came to visit again one day, so we went to the laundry and the way she explain it to me, I didn't think it would do for me, because I like my clothes clean. I rubbed them. She said, "They'll wash itself." And I couldn't think of putting all the clothes together in one machine. See that water gets hot, and you can let it stay in there as long as you want it. And I still rubbed them. I rubbed them from the first water, and I put them through the wringer too, to keep them in the tub of hot water. And then I turned the washer on, and it would do the work itself. And then I'd get them out; boy they'd come clean too. Bleach, that's when I started using bleach. And then they called it "bluing." You need a few drops in the rinsing water, and they'd come clean. From that time on, I've been taking my clothes to the laundry. I never had to do the other again.

We called it the steam laundry. And then after that, when these other washers came in where you don't turn nothing. And I didn't think that would work, get the clothes clean. But it sure does. Yes, it does, and you can change water too, if you want to. They charge by the hour. So ever since then they done away with the steam laundry; I started taking my clothes to the automatic laundry. I find it easier, and it's better than the way that will take a lady all day to do her laundry.[10]

Besides its use as laundry bleach, bluing, along with castor oil and Vicks VapoRub, were mid-twentieth-century home remedies. Vaseline, another household necessity, found a new use by Kiowa horn doctors who treated pneumonia by a procedure known in Western medicine as thoracentesis, inserting a tap in the pleural area between the chest wall and lungs to drain excess fluid. Patients were treated by making incisions in the abdomen and placing a hollowed-out cow horn over the cut to suck out the fluid. Odlepaugh was known for fashioning cow horns for Peyote doctors to treat pneumonia and blood clots. Gus Palmer Sr. once described how his father-in-law treated him for pneumonia with this technique (see Kracht 2017, 131–33; 2018, 244). In his youth Weiser contracted pneumonia and was treated by Kiowa Jim. When the country doctor made a house call to check on him, he was amazed by his rapid recovery. Upon learning details of the procedure, he suggested ditching the cow horn in favor of a sterilized Vaseline jar; instead of sucking with the horn, he recommended wood alcohol and cupping. Henrietta describes the operations performed with brown glass:

> I'll tell you how they do that. They suck the blood out; they have a horn, made out of a cow horn. I saw Grandfather [Odlepaugh] make one, one time. . . . And then they used it to get blood out. They claimed that when that bad blood gathers, it gives you a headache. And they use some kind of a bottle, not just a regular glass bottle, a dark-looking bottle. But he always had a piece of it. And then he'll get the horn and cut the skin around with the horn, hold the horn like that, and make a little round thing, then he'll cut with a glass. He has these glasses in hot water too, don't have to be cool off if you use them. Then you cut, and then he

used that sinew he'd chewed. That's why I know these things. I'm a good listener, and maybe I like to look; I like to watch to see what's going on. So I was watching him, and he had that sinew soaked in water. He'd cut up about so much of it, and he set soaked in the water. Washed it and then he chewed it. He chewed it until it just got kind of soft, that sinew. And then washed it back in the water, washed it back in there. And then he treat; he done that to my grandmother [Kol-an-on-da-mah]. He cut her head, and he'd put that thing over it, got the sinew out of the water after it's washed again. And he put it in his mouth; of course he rinsed it out. He put it in there, stuck that sinew against the horn with his tongue. I said, "How do you put that thing there?" He said, "Well, you just feel around with your tongue and just press it on there." And make that thing hold. It would hold for so long, and it would suck the blood out. And he would turn the horn over and just kind of scoop that blood out, and he'd pour the blood in a can. He rinse that with water, and he'd clean that horn again to do the next side. They say it was a sure cure for pneumonia. Even the doctor allow, I heard one time.

That old man, Weiser's dad? He used to do that to himself. . . . This doctor that lived over there at Alden. That old Alden historic site, two or three miles from there. There was a general store there too. And it was just kind of small place, but they had a doctor there, a country doctor. They had a church there, just small buildings of this and that. A blacksmith shop, cotton gin, and all that. My husband [Weiser] was a little boy, and he got sick. Pneumonia. So [Kiowa Jim] doctored him that way. Then when the doctor came and saw him, he said, "He had pneumonia, but he's getting over it. How did you do that?" And he saw the marks on his chest. And the old lady [Fannie], she kind of understood the white language, and she told him how they did it. And he said, "Well, that's good. But let me tell you. I think this will do better if you don't have the horn." So those little Vaseline jars. Old-time Vaseline jars, little bitty, about the size of a Vicks mentholated, an ointment that you put on for colds. He said, "You can sterilize those Vaseline bottles. They come in a clear bottle. Wash them out real good. Sterilize them, and soak them in warm water. And you can use that to cut yourself and get the blood out." And that's the way he did. And he used wood alcohol. Said not allowed to buy it, but he gave him a permit. I saw that too. . . .

Just anybody can do that, with horn. But this Dr. Weiser, that's where my husband got his name. Dr. Weiser, a German doctor, comes out in a buggy; he's a country doctor at Alden. And that's what he told them to do, and that's the way they've been doing it [since]. And I was watching the old lady [Fannie] do that, and she had a wire, and she dip that in wood alcohol in a smaller bottle. And she'd dip that in there, and she struck a match and stuck it in the bottle, and right fast she put that bottle on the body, like that. And it just held, and you could see that blood going inside that Vaseline jar, clear; you could see it. They do to themselves, some of them.

And then she'd scoop that blood from her body and pour it out in a can and rinse the bottle again and clean it out and then use it. Well, she had two, one time about three or four bottles they could use. So that's the way they'd do. Some women do that to another lady. It can suck the blood in a back and in the chest, for pneumonia, and sure brings them out of it. Some people were talking about a lady, that her leg was swelling. They didn't know what was wrong, so she used it; one of the ladies did that. And they said it was where the blood comes into a lump and stops the circulation. Blood clot. They suck somewhere else, not at the same place, but suck just kind of a little ways from there, and then some of the blood starts circulating through. And then they get alright. My aunt was having problems with her leg when it start swelling and my Grandma tried that, and she got okay. She started walking alright. And they say it's good for arthritis too; when your legs aching in the joints somewhere, they'll get that bad blood out, and then you'll get okay.[11]

Although Odlepaugh, Kol-an-on-da-mah, Kiowa Jim, and Fannie practiced indigenous therapy and followed older traditions, they encouraged Henrietta and Weiser to attend church.[12] Like other converts, they amalgamated traditions into an indigenized version of Christianity (see Kracht 2018). Raymond recalls his uncle Rev. Cecil Horse horn doctoring Weiser's temple, and he also watched Grandma Fannie doctor, though he cannot recall the patient's name. He adds, "I remember that we kids used to tease each other when one acted up. BEHAVE! I'll put the horn to you!" Later in life individuals with hangovers were taunted with this expression.[13] Horn doctors continued to practice into the twenty-first century, though today most are gone. Henrietta's cousin Lorena "Ella Faye" Bigbow Horse (1922–2018) was one of the last traditional Kiowa healers.

## Editing

Raymond, Lisa, and I initially agreed that Henrietta's manuscript needed some light editing—adjusting punctuation, standardizing spellings, removing capitalization—but decided not to distort her voice by correcting grammar or rearranging the stories. Realistically, editing Henrietta's notebook became problematic because the narrative is fractured and repetitive. Chronologically, her stories hopscotch between home, school, and church life and are broken up by lists of relatives, neighbors, and members of Saddle Mountain Church. Thus, it's unclear when she attended different schools or lived with different relatives. Another issue besides the fragmented stories is that some of them are incomplete. Perhaps these problems are attributed to the creation of the narrative; switching between black and blue ink eleven times suggests that Henrietta wrote intermittently. Shelley Tongkeamha lived with her grandparents in the 1980s and said that Henrietta favored a pen with blue and black cartridges. I suggest that each session is designated by color and that her narrative was written in no fewer than eleven sittings.[14]

While grappling with editorial concerns, I recalled my last visits with Henrietta in early June 1993, toward the end of a monthlong field season that began with Clifton's unexpected death and funeral. Normally, Kiowa mourning customs preclude social interactions following the death of a close relative, but Henrietta graciously accepted my visits and granted my request for tape-recorded interviews because she said Clifton had been fond of me. Perhaps cognizance of her pending death also motivated her to deviate from tradition by sharing some stories with me.[15] During the interviews Henrietta talked about boarding schools, religion, and her grandparents. After comparing the interview transcriptions to her written memoirs, I determined that both narratives are concordant. However, the interview data are more detailed.

Christopher Teuton (2010, xvi) observes that Native communication involves "oral impulses" and "graphic impulses." These impulses "build on the premise that oral discourses are living forms of cultural knowledge, kept alive in the memory of members of a group; graphic discourses record tradition for posterity, to live beyond the lives of those who record them." Oral impulses are spoken traditions transmitted person to person and within communities, whereas graphic impulses are "lasting formats" like Haudenosaunee wampum belts, Diné sandpainting, and Mesoamerican writing systems. Teuton proposes that Native signification also involves "critical impulses" that balance oral and graphic impulses; "when the oral and the graphic are in conversation with one another the critical impulse flourishes." Neither form should dominate the other (32, 55). Significantly, critical impulses involve multiple formats: "an authoritative oral story may be counteracted with another oral story or with a graphic text; a graphic text may be undercut by another graphic text or with an oral story," thereby creating "fluid stability," the "life force of cultural production and survivance" (xviii).

Inspired by Teuton's notion of "critical impulses," I decided to interweave Henrietta's oral voice from the tape-recorded interviews into her memoirs to augment the narrative; such instances are identified in endnote citations as "H. Tongkeamha, interview." Other editorial changes involved rearranging paragraphs, sentences, and clauses and removing repetition to create a fluid narrative. Genealogical data not essential to her stories were omitted. Best judgement was used to maintain the chronology of her life story between 1918 and 1936. In all instances ampersands were changed to "and," missing punctuation was added, and periods were changed to commas or vice versa. Proper nouns were capitalized, and capitals were removed for regular nouns. Her spellings for relatives differ from spellings used elsewhere: Sate-tan-ta (a.k.a. Set'aide or Satanta), her great-grandfather; Kol-an-on-da-ma (alt. Kol-an-on-da-mah), her grandmother; and Ole-paugh (alt. Odlepaugh), her grandfather. I have retained her spellings. Numbers and some abbreviations were standardized: "5" to "five," "2nd" to "second," "yrs" to "years," "de" to "delicious," "am" to "amazing," and "Gparents" to "grandparents." Other abbreviations remain unaltered: "thru," "'cause," "nite," "Gpa," and "Gma." Instances where markers for past tense /-ed/ or plurality /-s/ are missing were unchanged. The possessive marker /'/ was added when necessary. Two words were conjoined, as in "wayside" and "anytime," or hyphenated, as in "square-shape." Occasional endnotes give backstories and identify people and places; box brackets denote missing words or correct spellings and dates. Although several discrepant dates exist in the memoirs, memories are more important than dates, as noted by Margo Tamez (2016, 240): "For indigenous peoples, place, memory, and oral histories are often more relevant and crucial than dates, so finding a balance between oral traditions and Western historical methods is complex."

## "This Is the Story of My Life"

I am Henrietta Apayyat Tongkeamha, a Kiowa Indian. I am a descendant of Chief Sate-tan-ta, White Bear. The great granddaughter of Sate-tan-ta. My Grandpa Ole-paugh is the son of Sate-tan-ta. Grandpa Ole-paugh married Kol-an-on-da-ma, which means "Buffalo Foot Print." Had five daughters and one son. Hattie Ole-paugh was the oldest daughter; second daughter, Ruth Ole-paugh; third, my mother, Lula; fourth, Grace; fifth, Betty Ole-paugh. I don't remember their son's name. He passed away at young age. My mother, Lula, is the granddaughter of Sate-tan-ta. All the relatives I remember on my mother's side of family are descendants of Chief Sate-tan-ta, White Bear. Sate-tan-ta's father is Red Te-pee. Sate-tan-ta White Bear's [wife] is Akeen-tay. Akeen-tay is mother of Gpa Ole-paugh. My mother, Lula, married Fremont Apayyat. My father, Fremont, is the son of Susie Tenegooah and Albert Oyebi. Father Fremont had three brothers and one sister: Tom, Winston, and Fred Oyebi. Aunt Lizzie Oyebi. My parents are enroll at Kiowa Agency at Anadarko, Oklahoma. I was the first child born to them. I was born May 18, 1912, in Kiowa County near Gotebo, Oklahoma. I have one sister, Margaret Apayyat, and brother, Bruce Kinney Apayyat.

My mother Lula Ole-paugh's Indian name is Taye-ga-day, meaning standing far away. Each Indian given name has a meaning, or a war deed, or something that happen. My Gma Susie's mother was half-Cheyenne. When I was a little girl, my Indian name was Cheyenne. Because my great grandmother was half-Cheyenne. Later my grandmother Kol-an-on-da-ma change my Indian name, so it was Zone-kout-i. Meaning going thru the pine. My sister Margaret's Indian name is Ah-kie-gape, meaning hit by the enemy. We all have Indian names, and down thru fifth generations, some don't [have] Indian names. So we give names to some of our children from our relatives that are decease, and the relative sometime give him or her name to a grandchild. Some of these Indian names are handed down. My father gave his Indian name, A-paye-yah, meaning they roped him. My other son, Clifton Tongkeamha, has the name Tong-kea-am ha, meaning Coming Out of Water. The Indian Agency try to spell some of the Indian names the way they sound. They translate the Indian names or they enrolled each individual at the Indian Agency in Anadarko, Oklahoma. And my son James Tongkeamha has the name of his father's uncle. His father, Weiser, had the name of his uncle Pue-soye-hey. Pue-soye-hey. Meaning a blue object. Up to the time my other children don't have Indian name.[16] Mother Lula passed away 1916 [July 27, 1918]. We were all small. I was almost four years. Margaret was three years. Bruce was two years. We hardly remember her (Mother). The only way I remember her was when she was sick in bed. And I remember when she was all covered in bed, and lot of people were sitting around in the room. I was sitting by Grandpa [Odlepaugh] on the floor. Everyone was sitting on the floor, and the rest I don't remember.

Those that knew her have nice things to say about her, and it makes me glad to know she was my mother. Some of her friends are Jennie Haumpy Horse, Adelaide Tonemah Little Chief, Bell Kicking Bird, Mamie Horse, and Richenda Toyebo. They also said she was beautiful, and I know she is because I have her picture. My mother and Aunt Ruth and Grace all went to school at Rainy Mountain Boarding School. Aunt Hattie did not go to school. When mother passed away, my other grandparents, the Oyebis, came after me to live with them. My sister, Margaret, and brother, Bruce, lived with the Ole-paughs. Gpa Albert and Gma Susie lived on Gma Susie's allotted land, west of Apache, Oklahoma. Seven miles west, and one and a half miles north. They lived in a large five-room house. On their farm was a big red barn, a chicken house, and other small buildings. Aunt Lizzie and her husband, Thomas Auchiah; my dad; Uncle Tom; Winston; and Fred all lived with Gpa and Gma Oyebi. I was the only child in this home.

The first grandchild in this home, I know that something was different. And a reason for me to live with the Oyebis; they were all good to me, took good care of me. Getting adjusted to everything in Gma and Gpa's home was a joy. I know they love me. But I had sad and lonely time. Seeing other children with mothers. Living with my grandparents, the Oyebis, was not new to me. I recall being there off and on. And I knew them as my grandparents.

Gpa and Gma's place is home, known as Catt Spring, that runs all thru seasons a pretty clear spring water. Grandma Susie's home was beautiful, a large five-room house and a big red barn, a chicken house, and other small buildings. Locus trees planted on east to south side of house. The spring of clear water that never run dry. The water is clear and beautiful. They carry water in buckets to the house for family use, drinking water, etc. No hot water for dishes or for bath. They have to heat it on stove to wash dishes or for bath. They go into lot of trouble, but it was the best living. On the west was a peach, apricots, and plum orchard that bear fruit every springtime. I eat fruit to my heart's content. They also had horses, cows, and chickens. My uncles feed the horses and cows and milk the cows. I like to watch the horses eat grain, especially when they chew corn. I am always around to watch them milk the cows. They milk the cows by hand. Uncle Winston and Tom put a bucket under the cow's milk bag and go to work. They can get a gallon or more from each cow while milking the cows. The cows seem contented standing still and chewing away. Gma strain the milk thru a clean white rag into a large bowl. The milk sits all nite will form thick cream of top of milk. Gma skim the cream off the milk, and when she get enough she shakes it into butter in a small syrup basket. They take turns shaking or churning the butter. They later bought a churn, which can then turn by hand. Gma also made homemade cheese. When Gma gathers eggs, I help her. During spring season Gpa Albert plant garden with the help of my uncles. And they work in the garden all the time until it is ready to pick. Gpa and Gma pick what they want out of the garden when it is ready and take it to the spring to wash fresh onions, radishes, and etc. I am proud to say my Gpa and Gma are workers, also my uncles.

Gma do her laundry by the spring under the shade trees. Gpa builds the fire to heat water for the laundry. My uncles help fill the big pot with water, and they keep the fire going to keep the water hot. When water is hot, Gma start her laundry washing whites first, rubbing each garment on a rub board. She put all the whites in the pot of hot water to boil awhile, and she rubs her colored clothes. She go thru this twice. And the whites are ready to take out of pot to rub again, rinse in clean water. Wring each garment by hand to get water out of each garment. And they are ready to hang on clothes line to dry. She use lye for whites, and they really turn out white. She takes a break at noon, have to fix dinner for the family.[17] And after dinner she proceed until all her laundry is done. Doing laundry in the old day is nearly all-day work. I spend my time playing in the water nearby. I catch little minnows or crawfish in shallow water, put them in a fruit jar, and watch them swim around.

Gma Susie's relatives come to visit now and then. In the good old days relatives and family spend a few days together just visiting. When some of these relatives come to visit, Gma and Gpa would butcher a beef some time, and everybody have a good time visiting and eating together. Sometime when relatives come, they get a beef from the leaseman. They cut the meat, slice it, and hang it on poles to dry. They cook some on open fire. Also they clean and wash the bote in the spring water. Slicing meat to dry is a process. The beef is butchered. The women cut all the meat from the bone, which comes in large chunks. The meat is now slice; a large piece of meat can be cut in two. To begin, the meat is sliced it in the center, and, as it is slice, the meat is rolled out in the palm of hand. The meat is slice as it is rolled out in hand, and it keeps on getting longer as it thins out. And it is ready to hang on long poles that has already been set up. Two uprights and one across. The poles are space about nine to ten feet apart. Several poles can be set up. When meat is hung on the poles in the sun, after a while they turn the meat over until it is good and dry. It takes about two or three day in hot sun to dry. They never butcher on rainy or cloudy day. The meat some time get so dry it crumble into fine pieces when it is stored in the cowhide bag. Dried meat cook with salt meat or pork is a treat. It is boil together until tender. Relatives enjoy these times together. The meat is shared with the neighbors, friends, and relatives. The Smokeys or the Berrys would come sometime and spend few days together. The neighbors also came when a beef is butchered. The neighbors are Uncle John Aunko and family. Aunt Sadie Ahpeahtone and family. The Stumbling Bears, the Little Chiefs. The Chainos. The Frizzleheads. They visit each other. We also go to their home. I look forward to these times to play with the neighbor children.

During summer harvest my uncles and Dad help the white neighbors haul their wheat to Apache. They follow the thrasher; they camp near the place where they cut and thrash wheat. Gma checks on her boys to see if they have everything they need. I rode to the field with her. I think she was more worried about them getting hurt on the job. The big thresher look like a large animal making lot of noise. The white neighbors in those days were friendly and nice. One day they were threshing at our nearest neighbor, Mr. Hill. Gma and I walk to their place. We came there right at noon here. The ladies were busy waiting on tables; the men were eating, and they were serving them. Mrs. Hill ask us to sit with the ladies and eat. Oh boy! They had all kind of food desserts. It was a very good meal. Guess Gma had it time right. Gma and Gpa doesn't speak English. But they have a way of understanding the white man, and the white man understand the Indians. So they get along pretty well. The white man invite an Indian in his house, and the Indians also invites the white man into his house to talk about a land lease deal or buying beef or horse.

One year during World War I, Uncle Tom went into U.S. Army service, and when he left home it was a sad parting for the family.[18] I know Gma miss him very much. Because when she got lonesome for him, she will cry one day when she had one of lonely, sad moments. She was sitting under the arbor crying. I was sad also because I did not want her to cry. I picked some honeysuckles and put one on each one of her fingers. She looked at me and smile. I was glad to see her smile. I play with the honeysuckles when they bloom; they are so pretty. When I put one on each finger they make my fingers look long. There was a long patch on east side of Gma's house, and they had honeysuckles planted all across the porch.[19] There were also trees planted east of the house, and on the south side was trees also. Makes the place look beautiful. I don't know how long Uncle Tom was in service, and one day he came home. It was a big welcoming home for him. Relatives and friends were at Gma and Gpa home to welcome him home. They had a Peyote meeting and a big feast for him; lots of people came. Gma and Gpa butchered a beef. I know Gma and Gpa was very happy their son came home. On occasion they had Peyote meetings, such as birthdays and holidays, Thanksgiving, Easter, or New Year. And when someone is sick in the family. They put up a te-pee [tipi]. And get the medicine man to doctor the patient. When they prepare to put up a te-pee. The relatives come to help two or three days ahead of time, and they all work together getting wood for the fire that they keep up all night or help butcher a beef for the feast. They usually butcher near the creek under a shade tree. And also clean the bote and wash it in the creek. They cut the meat off the bone to get ready to cook. And they slice it to hang on the poles to dry. They enjoyed these times together.

Gma Susie took me in the te-pee one time when they had a meeting. She fix a pallet for me behind her where she sat. I didn't sleep for a long time. I sat up to watch what was going to happen or take place. The reason for taking me in the meeting was me being sick. But I didn't feel that bad because I wanted to watch. The people I saw in the meeting are Little Chief and wife, Frizzlehead and wife, Mark Auchiah and wife, Stumbling Bear and wife, Ned Brace, Noble Starr, Old Man Yeahque and wife. Some Apache tribe I don't know.[20] Old Man Yeahque was my doctor.

He chewed a peyote button and took it out of his mouth and rolled it in the palm of his hand several times and gave it to me to eat. I held it in my hand and didn't want to eat it. Gma urge me with her encouraging word that I would be alright. So, yak! I had to get it down, and it wasn't tasty. Later I finally went to sleep. In the morning a lady brought in a bucket of water for everyone to drink, and after a prayer that was led by the lady that brought in the water, everyone drink water and then the breakfast was also brought in. A bowl of poach corn, a bowl of prunes, dried pounded beef jerky in a pan mix with sugar and tallow. Each bowl of food is pass around. And each person in the meeting for breakfast take one or two spoonful to eat. The pounded dried beef is taken out in the pan by handful. Gma took one handful for me and for herself. What I saw in the meeting was people sitting around in circle. The te-pee is set facing east is the custom. The chief or the priest sits on the west side in the middle. And in the center of the te-pee a mound in shape of a moon is made. And in the center on the mound is place a large peyote button.

The mound is shaped smooth and perfect. The members pray and sing and thru the meeting, they eat the peyote. They sing in partners and beat the small drum, and the other shake the gourd while they sing. A man is selected to keep the fire going all nite. Every one sit up all thru the meeting. No one sleeps until the next day. Inside of te-pee is warm and comfortable. All sit on the ground, which is comfortable with pallets and pillows to sit on. After breakfast they rest or sleep awhile until dinnertime. The dinner is prepared by the women that came to help. The visitors also come to eat, and the neighbors all have a good time eating and visiting. Some stay for supper, and some relatives stay over until the te-pee is taken down and everything put away until next time. It seem to be lot of work. But I know people enjoy these times. I get to play with the children, and it was fun for me.

During the time I lived with my grandparents, we go visit my other grandparents, the Ole-paugh. They also come to visit from Saddle Mountain. I get to see my sister and my brother, Bruce. Gma and Gpa also visit the Smokeys at Verden. We travel a long way in wagon or buggy. But people don't seem to be in a hurry those day. We spend a few days and come back home. We start very early to go to Verden, and by sundown we get there. Coming home was the same. They stop on the wayside near a creek to give the horses rest and give them water. Gma fix lunch under a shade tree, and we eat. And after lunch we are on our way again.

One day I had my first train ride, and I was thrill to my bones. Uncle Tom took us to the depot at Apache, a train stop. He took us in the buggy, and we went on to Verden on the train. It was a smooth ride. The seats were soft and comfortable. I enjoyed it very much. Gpa [Enos] Smokey was waiting for us in his car at the Verden depot. Few Indians own cars in those days. They know when the train arrive. Some time we go by train to Anadarko Agency and ride on the taxi to the agency. It is always a joy for me to ride the train. It wasn't often, but it was good. And one day I had my first car ride in the year 1920. Mr. Yoder, a white neighbor, is a leaseman for Gma and Gpa. Mr. Yoder want them to sign a new lease and told Gpa he would take us to Anadarko to the agency to sign their lease. Gma got ready and also got me ready. I remember it was very cold that day. Gpa said, here he comes, we were all ready. Gma took some blankets to wrap us up. Mr. Yoder had a 1920 Model T Ford with side curtains. I couldn't hardly wait for that ride. Finally got started and away we went. We could see only to the front because of the side curtains. It was a wonderful car ride. It was so good. I went to sleep coming home. Gma pile blankets on me. I wanted to stand up and look out, but she wouldn't let me. It was cold but a good ride.

They go by wagon to Apache to buy their supply of groceries. It wasn't often, but it was always good to go to Apache town. It is always a slow and hot ride during summer. No highways, the ride was bumpy. But I can actually sleep while we are on our way by Apache because it is slow. They buy groceries in a store by the name of Warner's Grocery. We see other Indians in there. They visit awhile talking to people. Gpa park the horses and wagon behind Warner's store in the alley. They buy a large supply of groceries. When they get thru buying groceries, they go to other stores down the street, a dry goods store, a drug store, and sometimes to a café. I was also thrilled when we ate in the café. One time I ate hamburger, and when we go in the drug store to buy ice cream. That is the most happy time of my life, but it is not very often, and drinking strawberry pop is a thrill of my life. I looked forward to those times. I found happiness living with my Gma and Gpa.

My Aunt Lizzie, Uncle Winston, and Tom went to a public school. The name of the school is Mountain Home. The public schools had a name in those days. They call them day school. It is about one and a quarter mile west from Gma's place. They walk to school every day. One day or evening, we were outside and they coming home from school, and we heard Uncle Winston crying. Gma waited for them to get home. She asked him what was wrong. He said a white boy fought him and made him cry. Gpa had just come in from a country store on a single buggy. He was unloading. When he got thru, Gma got in the buggy. I was right behind her. She drove toward the school. We met the children. The boy that had a fight with Uncle Winston ran when he saw Gma. She got off the buggy with her whip. The boy crawl under the fence, and his shirt got caught under the barbwire. Gma gave him a whipping he never forgot. He cried and all the other kids were crying also. We drove back home. After all the years Mr. Earl Meekly told my husband, Weiser, that he never forgot the whipping my Gma gave him. Besides, Meekly was our neighbor at the old place south of town.

I enjoyed living with my grandparents. I was happy knowing that Gma cared for me. Gpa Oyebi was also a kind Gpa. I don't remember what age I first went to school. They took me to a boarding school. The Kiowa school was Rainy Mountain, near Gotebo, Oklahoma, in Kiowa County. All the students were Kiowa. Mother Lula and her sisters also went school there.[21] I was scared because I did not know how to speak English. Most of the small children didn't know how to understand or speak the white man language. I was very lonesome when they left me. I got acquainted with some of the girls, and it wasn't so bad. All the girls dress the same. Blue denim dress, black stockings, and black-lace shoes. The big girls comb our hair; we have pigtails with ribbons. My classmates were Grace Tompson, Helen Tonetigh, Ethel Satepeahtaw, Louise Brace, and Scott Tonemah. We were in the kindergarten. Our teacher's name was Miss Hartsah. Our girl's matron's name was Miss Paytae. Our principal's name was Mr. Bishop. Other girls I remember went school there are Nellie Doyah Satepahoodle, Mattie Daugomah Hainta, Josephine Tompson Tsoodle, Olive Gilbert, Eunice Tonkebo, S. Horse, Mary Chaddleson, Opal Yeahque, Jennie Chanate, Mary Ahauty, and Jennie Giemausaddle. Others I don't remember. Before I went to school there during the time, mother went school there. I heard about some of the old Kiowas went school there, Oliver Tanedoah, Corn Bread Tanedoah, Jennie Haumpy Horse, Mamie Tsoodle Wolf, Mamie Horse, Helen Paukie, Pearl Tonecatt, Alice Chanate, Walter Kokom, Chevers Toppah and his brother Moses Toppah, Carl Tofpi, and many others.

The parents come to visit the children on wagons or buggy. Sometime they camp east of the school in the pasture over the weekend. They had their annuity payments. They all came from the north, from the south to the north. In camps, and then the students can go there while they're camped there during the day, or what time they get off, out of school, or from their details. They can go and visit and report back to the building. So each child, even a baby, got an annuity payment. I don't remember how much it was.[22] My grandparents, the Ole-paughs, used to camp. They took the children to town at Gotebo. There was a [Boake's] general store one-quarter mile east of the school. Some of the students walk over there. Gotebo was a little town north of the school. About seven or eight miles. They had a few stores. Two dry goods stores, drug store. Three grocery store. Variety store, café, barber shop, a silent movie theater, a post office, and a bank. Also a funeral home. On Saturday everybody around near Gotebo go to shop. There were few Indians that own cars. The general store managed by Mr. Boake charge thirteen cents a gallon for gas. When he credit, he charge twenty cents a gallon. Indians were furious for him to charge twenty cents a gallon. 'Cause he was. I remember when gas was thirteen cents a gallon.[23] And I think, on credit, he would charge them twenty cents a gallon. The few that had cars, not everybody had [cars]. They had those long [gas pumps]; they wind them up somehow. And then they turned

7. Boake's Store, one mile east of Rainy Mountain School, May 2018. Photograph by Benjamin Kracht.

it on, when you paid for it in cash, let's see, thirteen cents a gallon or fifteen cents a gallon. But when you credit, you want him to put it on a charge, you twenty cents a gallon. And still some of them thought it was too much, 'cause their money wasn't there.

And then the store, that empty store, they call him Mr. Boake. And he had a general store; it [has] everything. He has hardware; he has material; he has some clothing, like the men's clothing, shirts, and shoes and socks. That's where Mr. Boake first start selling shawls. And he has harness for the horses, and he has everything. He has groceries, meat, salt, bacon, and all, every item of the groceries. He had all that. Material. And lots of people credit over there. They pay during the payment; the annuity paid it. And they paid good too, I think.[24]

I went to school at Rainy Mountain for a few months, and one day my uncle Tom and Gpa Oyebi came after [me] because Gma Susie was getting sick and getting worse. I didn't know how serious her sickness was. I was not old enough to know the seriousness of sickness. Some of the relatives were there with her. She has been sick for some time. The doctor told the folks she had cancer. They did all they could for her. Took her in Peyote meeting, believing a medicine man would cure her. After everything fail to help her, she passed away in the home. Another sad time for me. Friends and relatives stay to help. She was buried at Cache Creek Indian Cemetery west of Apache, Oklahoma. Some of the relatives stopped several days in our home. When there is a death in a family, most of the relatives stay to help and do what they can for the family. They put [me] in boarding school at Rainy Mountain again. During summer vacation Rainy Mountain Kiowa School was closed. About 1923 or 1924 [June 30, 1920].

Gpa Oyebi; Aunt Lizzie; her husband, Thomas Auchiah; Uncles Tom, Winston, Fred; and Dad all stayed and lived in the house. My other grandparents, the Ole-paughs, came after me to live with them at Saddle Mountain. My sister, Margaret, and brother, Bruce, were living together again. I miss my Gma Susie very much. Aunt Lizzie would come after us sometime, and we stay for a few days with them. About a year or two later, Gpa Oyebi married again; he married a one-half Kiowa and Apache lady. They later moved to her place near Fort Cobb. Aunt Lizzie and the rest lived at the old home place. When Gma Susie passed away, it wasn't a home like it use to be. Dad also got married again to Pearl Doyebi Kotay. Dad and Pearl's marriage didn't last too long. I don't remember when they separated, and he later married Aunt Sarah Long Horn. They made their home with Sarah's mother and stepfather. Aunt Sarah was my mother's first cousin. She was our aunt, and she became my stepmother. Brother Herman Lee Oyebi and Evelyn Mahzole Chelepah was born to them. They lived at Sedan, a small place south of Mountain View.

And the following school term, they took me to Riverside Boarding School north of Anadarko, Oklahoma. My cousin Mary Chaddleson was also going to school at Riverside. The boarding school students are mix Indians, Kiowas, Creeks, Caddos, Wichitas. We all made friends. Riverside was like a military school; we have a roll call. Each one of us had a number, and we answer to our numbers. We fall in line for everything: going to breakfast, lunch, and dinner, also to class and to church. We also drill in the mornings, also on Saturdays. We fall in line for inspections on Sunday mornings before marching to church. We all wear the same color of clothing. And black high-top shoes with shoelace and black stockings. We say Indians want to take time about everything. But like, when we're in a dormitory, the bell will ring; the matron would have to get up at a certain time. Then everybody have to get out of bed. It's just like the military. We rise at six in the morning to the sound of the alarm. And then right there, as soon as you get up, you start fixing your bed. Smooth out your sheets; make your bed roll, 'cause the matron will go in there, and she'll check all the beds. If there's one not made right, she'll make you do it over. And then another bell rings, and everybody have to be through with the beds, with their bed, and go down the washroom. And then, of course, the bathroom, the washroom, you comb your hair, brush your teeth. We had to be on time for everything. There are three companies A, B, C. C Company are little girls; B Company was middle girls; A Company are the big girls. I was in the C Company. So we'd go by numbers, like A or C Company or B Company. And then we're in a group, and then we'd go by numbers at Rainy Mountain. That's where I first learned that. Atwater Onco was telling me all that. He should know all that 'cause I think his dad went to school over there.[25] And we went by numbers, 1, 2, 3, 4, 5. Each girl had a number, up to how many girls there were there. I don't remember my number at Rainy Mountain, but I remember it at Riverside. My number was 89. So suppose you drop your sweater, and they pick it up and check the number, and it was 89. They say, "89, here's your sweater. Hang it up." So go and do it. Even our shoes are labeled with numbers. So we don't get mixed up that way.[26]

Everything was in order. There were shower days too, so it's like every day, every day for one group go in; the next group goes, change about like that. So that's what goes on. And on Sundays we wore the same color uniform. Uniforms made out of, we called them uniforms, they made out of blue serge material. They all alike. They pretty too. I was proud of mine. And the colors are red and blue. And they're also labeled with numbers. And then Sunday morning, we'd have to be through by the tap of the bell; that's the whole school. That's the whole school. They all fall in line and we, then the principal comes out to inspect us. We must have our fingernails clean, we must have our shoes polished, we must have our hair combed, neat, and our uniforms. We're in line, two rows, each company, A, B, C Company. Alright, the principal will come, start from the A, and the matron will follow, and he'll look at us in the front row, and then he'll come back and check the back row, and then he'll come down and check this row. Go up the end, turn around, come back end, and check the back. And if there is ribbon hanging or your hair hanging out of line, the matron will point out to that student, and she'll have to go in the washroom and straighten it. Or her shoes, if they're not polished, they'll point at her shoes. The matron is following. She'll send the girl in, [and] the boys is the same way. And when we tell about it, they used to say, that's military school. Well, I guess it was; everybody had to march; we drill, we'd drill for exercise. And we exercised in the morning while the breakfast is being fixed. The A Company go out and do their exercise, stretch out our arms, had all kind of ways of exercise then. Then the B Company when the A Company is through. The B Company do the same thing. And then the C Company. We'd jump up and down; we do that too.[27]

After the girls are out of bed, there's a bell for the kitchen girls to march to the dining hall. And then another bell after everybody gets through in the washrooms, we'll all fall in line, just like military. And then another tap of bell, then we all marched to the dining hall. And then we eat; we all say a prayer together. And a prayer, a tap, a bell for the prayer. We know how long the prayer was, all the people saying prayer. And then we're through with that, and then we'd go ahead and eat. And then, I think it's about thirty minutes or forty-five minutes, another tap, and everybody has to be through from the table, push their chairs under the table, and get up and march out. And then later on, just a few, a few minutes later, another tap of bell at the building, and you start getting ready for school. And then the detail, the laundry girls go to their duty; the sewing girls, by that time, the kitchen girls are back.[28]

And they change about, have two groups of kitchen girls. It would have half a day school; one group would go and help in the kitchen, while the rest go to school. And then they change about like that, to every detail; they would go to school half a day. When classes dismissed, we'd report to our duties, and then the girls are on duty will come to the building and get ready and start their class. So it's just changing about like that. Everyday. When our group is released, then the other group comes out of class, and they finish the rest of the day on. And then their clothes are numbered too. The boy's clothing, we carry them in baskets; we carry them, the overalls, the pants, in one basket. We put them in their closet there, and they just go over there and pick out their clothes, when they're going to change. They're numbered, also the shirts, socks. Everything was numbered, so you can't be wearing anybody else's socks or shirt or pants.[29]

And all of the details I didn't care for are the laundry. They have a big, large washer, where all the overalls, they wear overalls those days. Some women wear slacks, like pants or jeans. They put them all in the washer and start the washer, and they go and put soap in there, and then the laundry matron will say, "Alright, they're ready to . . ." She'll turn the water on, and it drain; all the water will drain out of that; it's a great big washer. And then you just get a stick and pull their clothes out. And then you put in a rinse. You run clear water and put 'em in a tub again and run clear water, and then you rinse again. Let the water out; you put 'em in a basket, and we take them out on a line to hang. Each garment we hang on the line, no dryers. Ohhh, there were shirts and shirts, and there were pants and pants, socks, towels, sheets, everything. Kitchen towels, aprons, all those things have to washed at the laundry. The sewing room, there's girls that go to the sewing room, patching overalls, patching shirts, whatever that needs sewing; the girls do that. There was students that was detail for each. They were like laundry, then the cooks, and the kitchen. The kitchen are the waitress; the kitchen girls are two groups: some are waitress, some are help cook, the cook that works there. She's a cook. And then some work in a bakery, learn how to make bread. We have homemade bread all the time. And just sliced it, you know, homemade bread. And then the kitchen girls, I mean the cook and the bakery girls, and the waitresses, all of them. After everybody is through eating, well, they all get together and pick up the dishes from the table, several tables. On each table there is six students. Two on this side, each side, and one on the end. That's how tables are.[30]

I met Clara Griely Moonlight there at Riverside. She was in the A Company. She took care of me; she comb my hair, help me fix my bed, and etc. She was very kind for me. And I learned to love her and look forward for her help. Somehow she had compassion on me when I was small. She is a nice person. During holidays students can go home, and vacation time is always good to be home and with relatives. Vacation time I lived with Dad, Sarah, and Sarah's parents west of Sedan. Also my sister, Margaret, and brother, Bruce, we all lived together there. During school year they send me to a public school at Sedan.

Later we all went to Riverside, Margaret, Bruce, and me. I was in the sixth grade then. That was my second time.[31] It was first time for Margaret and Bruce. He play football for Riverside. Also basketball and baseball. He was a good ballplayer. He pitch for Riverside. Clara Griely Moonlight was not there anymore. (And later I still see her. She married Henry Moonlight. I never did forget her. I didn't see her often, but I'm always glad to see her whenever I can. I let her know that I appreciate her kindness.) I heard she went to Chilocco Indian School.[32] And sometimes later I and sister Margaret went to school at Fort Sill Indian. Cousin Minnie Spotted Horse also went to school at Fort Sill.

Riverside was more the same. Strick [Strict], get punish for talking our Indian language. They want us all to learn the English language, and if some of the girls, Kiowa girls, were together as friends, we'd talk Kiowa. And the other girls, Wichitas, Caddos, Delawares, whoever, would snitch, tell the matron. And then the matron would punish us. And oh, them punishments, some of them were kind of severe too.[33] The punishment is getting down on your knees, facing the wall, and holding both arms up for about twenty to thirty minutes. The girls stay on their side. The boys stay on their side. If a girl is seen talking to a boy on the campus, she get punish. They'd snitch on you, and you just have to take that punishment [like I did]. I was tired, on my knees, holding my arms, just trying to hold them up for fifteen minutes, twenty minutes. Boy, that's tiresome. Some of the girls they get paddled and some of the boys too.[34]

We had some activities, like the first Friday. The first Friday of the month, when students are all at the school. They register to come in, and we're all there. There's a limit of taking so many in, and after that no more can come in. And then we know how many girls are there already. And then some students are new, and they have a social gathering on the campus. All of us can meet on the campus and have games, to get acquainted with other students. Boys and girls, they allowed it that one time, to get acquainted with, make friends with each other. And we had chaperons there. And they pack a picnic lunch for us, or we'd go by and just pick up our lunch and go out on the campus and have our evening lunch. And then there was a social at night. So things like that went on, and they had a band.[35]

At Riverside we get to go to town twice a month. Two Saturdays was boys' town day, and two Saturdays was girls' town day each month. There was girls' town day on Saturday, and the next Saturday was boys' town day. And then the girls. And they take us in a great hay rake. It's a big, wide wagon, and they load hay in there. That's the kind of wagon they take us in. And not all the girls go, just some of the girls can go, those that got expense, shopping money, can go. But you would have to march around on the street together. Even have to stay as a group. A Company stays together, the B Company, and the C Company. All stay in their group. And then if a girl want something in a store, the rest of us would wait while she go in there and pick up what she want. We stand in line on the street to wait, and then we move on. It was a privilege to go in a store if we want anything. And then our money that we use to shop, we get checks. Like I and my sister, we had our mother's land when she passed away. We inherited her land, and it goes on our account. In the original account over here, and we can get ten dollars every time we'd go shopping. We had money every time we'd go shop. The lease money come in there to go on our account. We have account numbers in there. I remember my account number is H-103, over here at the BIA office. And they call you by number; they can hand you out a check. They say, "H-103, here's your check." And then the matrons get the checks at the school. They send them over, and then she has a list made, to call us that we can go shopping. So that's the money that we had. We had some oil lease on our land too. So we had spending money. The parents can come and take us to town sometimes. But we go in group. It's the same for the boys too. So those were the activities.[36]

After inspection [on Sundays] we all marched into the church. And the preacher that I remember used to come up there; he was a Baptist preacher. His name was Mr. Wilson. He was in charge of the Wichita mission north of Anadarko. He was up in age; he's probably gone, might have some family left. I think they had two daughters. So he comes on Sunday. We have church, and then afternoon we dismiss, and then we have our lunch. And then they took us on a picnic. And then the officers for each company. The C Company had an officer that chaperons them. And then the B Company had chaperon. So we'd go out and walk from Riverside way up in the woods, around there. And we'd been to a cemetery, a highway going west of Anadarko. The Wichitas are buried on a hill. We were up there. The matron took us up there one time; she was with us all the time. But then B Company and C Company. We'd go in groups but have a chaperon with us. They had an old cemetery. I don't see [how] they get up there with bodies. Way up on a hill and in the blackjacks. It was just north of Riverside on a hill up there. And that's where we went, and we'd just go walking on Sundays.[37]

And then we're on a team; we're involved in sports. I made the basketball team. I played forward with Maggie Teepaukie. I was slow I guess, but I hardly miss the basket. Other girls on team were Birdie Fergurson, a Kiowa from Mountain View; Lillie Little Chief-Chaino; Carrie Tappeto Gouladdle. Other girls on team were different tribes. It was fun playing basketball and etc. at Riverside. After school we practice basketball. We have team. We play other teams. I was telling these kids; we were talking about basketball. My granddaughters are big. I said, "I used to play basketball." And they started laughing, 'cause it was funny for me to be on a team. They said, "You did Grandma?" I said, "I sure did. I played basketball." They kept laughing. I said, "Well, what's funny anyway?" Then I said, "Listen, I was born a baby like you. And I growed, and I was a little girl like you, and I was a teenager at one time." I said, "Now look at me. I'm old." I said. And one of my small granddaughters said, "Oh, I thought you stayed that way all the time!"[38]

As I've mentioned before, we are glad to be home during summer vacation. From Sedan we travel on wagon or buggy to church at Saddle Mountain. Remember one day one of Dad's horse got sick while we were at the church. He walk the horse nearly all day, leading it around. Some of the boys at the church help him walk the horse. After church we started home to Sedan, and the horse didn't make it. When we were two and a quarter mile from home, the horse fell on the ground and couldn't get up. Dad drove the horse slow; he stops to let him rest, but he couldn't make it any further. It was dark now. He unhitch the other horse, got some of the harness off the other horse, and put the harness in the wagon. We all walk down the road. Dad was leading one horse. Brother Bruce and Herman rode the horse. Sarah carried Mahzole. It was warm and moonlight. We stop to rest two or three times before we got home. I didn't get tired. Next morning Gpa Steve Kotay and Dad went after the wagon. They never mention what they did with the dead horse. I don't remember how long Dad and Sarah were married. When Sarah and Dad separate, he lived with Aunt Lizzie again. And one day Dad took I, Margaret, and Bruce to Saddle Mountain to live with our grandparents, the Ole-paughs. Sometime I stayed with Aunt Lizzie and her husband at Saddle Mountain. But I felt contented at Gma and Gpa Ole-paugh's home.

After we quit going to Riverside, we were living again in their home, and we all went to public school at Saddle Mountain. I was teenage then. The name of the school was 101 District. The country school at Saddle Mountain was the last school I went to. I quit school at eighth grade. We had fun playing basketball. We walk one mile each day to school at Saddle Mountain. It is two miles after we walk back home. The neighbor Indian children went to school there. Uncle James Auchiah and his sister Mary and Hattie Auchiah, also another brother, Sam Auchiah.[39] Elsie and Alfred Wo-haw Gilbert, George and Eva Giemausaddle, Stecker Daugkie, Albert, Ellis, Rubie and Julie Aunko. Francis and Jennie Chanate, Maggie Reed Morrison, Rachel Reed, Daisy Reed, and Johnnie Reed. Several Indian people lived around Saddle Mountain, and they all went to church there. Margaret still didn't go to school. Our school bus was a covered wagon. I walk to the road and wait for the bus.

Some days are cold. And some time it rain while we are still in school, and we walk home in rain. Rain or snow we walk to school; we carry our lunch to school in small bucket or lunch pail. Gma fix us bacon sandwitche [sandwich], bake sweet potatoe, crackers, and cheeses. Gpa buy us lunch such as small can[ned] apples and ginger snaps, small cookies that I didn't like very much; they were bittersweet. We hardly had light bread for sandwiches. Bread was ten cents a loaf, but we didn't have it often. After school was a hungry time. When we get there, always few biscuits for us left over from dinner. I love Gma's hot biscuits. She cooks old-fashioned meals, but they are delicious. We had enough to eat, and we keep warm during the cold winter days.

One day when we were going home from school, there were cows and a mean bull. We heard the bull was mean, but was never near our way home. They were by the fence, and we were scared. And knowing that my sister, Margaret, was baptize. I told her to pray so no harm would come to us. The bull was going on making sounds. We were walking slow. My sister got on her knees and prayed. The cows walked away, and we walk home. One day my cousin that was going school with us had a red sweater on, and I took it off her because I was afraid the bull would see red and take after us. Things we did when we were small are funny today. Sometime after school we walk with the neighbor's children around the road and by Saddle Mountain Store. The Dodds children, the Ankos and Auchiahs children. Gpa and Gma don't like for us to walk around the road. It is three miles to our home, but we enjoy the company with neighbor children.

Sometime during the week Gpa Ole-paugh traveled to Mountain View to buy a supply of groceries. About twice or once a month, and he buy a supply that will last for quite some time, and with Gma's dried meats and fruit we never go hungry. The country store at Saddle Mountain have a good supply of groceries and etc. And it is always good to make a trip to the store. When Gpa make a trip to the store, we wait for his return because he bring each of us a sack of candy and box of Cracker Jack. He let us ride with him sometime, and he makes a trip south of the store to buy fresh butter and eggs. The farm family living there are Mr. Bond's family. White neighbors are nice and good to get along with. So everyone seemed to be contented. The things I like is traveling in wagon to Gotebo. When we are making the trip to Gotebo, Gma load quilts and blankets and prepare lunch. We start early, and by noon we are halfway to Gotebo. So they stop where there is a shady place to rest the horses and to have our lunch.

Gpa unhitched the horses to water then, while Gma fix our lunch, a picnic lunch that is already cook. We all sit on the ground to eat our lunch while the horses are grazing by the road. After lunch we travel again and finally make it to Gotebo. Going on long trip to Anadarko or Lawton, people stop on the roadside to have lunch. No cafés. But it was fun and good traveling. Sometime they built fire to make coffee or warm the lunch. On long ride I and my sister play awhile as we travel in the wagon, and we sleep awhile. The ride is rough and bump, but we enjoy the ride and sleep. Gma fix a pallet with her quilts and blankets, and that makes it a little comfortable. The buggy ride is nice and easy. Brother Bruce usually ride on his horse following us. When we travel to Gotebo, where Aunt Hattie lives; we usually spend a few days with her. Also to Aunt Ruth and Uncle Sherman Chaddleson. And we travel back to Saddle Mountain during the nite. Gma and Gpa tell stories. Bedtime stories about the old way, how they lived to survive. And they also told us Sane-day [Saynday] stories, a [legendary being] that roams.[40]

People in the old day are not in a hurry. They take their time in whatever they do. And take time traveling. Sometime they spend nite with friends or relatives. Sometimes I and sister Margaret stay with our Aunt Lizzie Auchiah. They make a home at Saddle Mountain too. They live north of the old Saddle Mountain Store. Her in-laws live southwest from them near the creek. The Indians lived thirty or forty miles from town. There are country stores where people buy their needs. It is amazing how the Indians stayed in good health. We don't see doctor often. In childbirth the midwife and neighbors help. No doctor. They have home remedies for colds and infection. Surgery is unhear of; once in a while, someone do have surgery. People are strong and healthy in those days because they work hard.

Gpa seems to know when the weather is changing during winter day. They have a wood heater and a wood cookstove and always had plenty of wood. He haul wood quite often. When his grandsons, Robert and Price Spotted Horse, came to our place, they help Gpa haul wood and help him chop wood. Gpa never used kerosene to build fire in the morning. He use his sharp pocketknife to slice kenlen [kindling] from a wooden box to start the kitchen stove and heater. During the very cold winter nite, he keeps the fire going all nite. We sleep warm. When weather is changing to some bad days, we stock wood on our screen porch and fill our water cans. Grandma covers the water with lids or canvas. So, when weather is bad, we don't go out to get wood and water. Grandma have food stored away, such as dried corn, dried meat, dried bote, dried plums. Mesquite beans and red berries for dessert. We always had something to eat.

One cold winter I wanted to play outside. There was snow and ice all over the ground. I got bored staying in the house, so I ask my sister Margaret to go with me. I made excuse to go after water at the spring, and Gma knew we didn't need water because we had all our cans and buckets fill with water. Sometimes we disobey to have little fun. I told Margaret to get her coat and stocking cap, and I gave her a water bucket for water. I also got a bucket, and we went outside. I wanted to skate on the frozen ice. It was downhill from our house to the spring. I ran and slide now and then. Margaret was screaming around; she was afraid to slide. Anyway, we got to the spring. And there was another downhill and a stream of water. We cross before we get to the spring. I slide down the little hill, and Margaret hand me the buckets. And I help her down; we walk to the spring and fill the buckets and started for house; we cross the little stream of water, and I climb the little bank or hill and told Margaret to hand me the bucket of water. We had two buckets. After I got the water on the hill, I slide down again and told Margaret I would help her up. I gave her a push behind with my hands and kept pushing until she reach the top. I pull her coat, and she slide all the way back down. She start screaming, and I thought it was funny. I told her I would get her up there this time, so I gave her push again and did the same thing here; she slide back down. She was also laughing and screaming. All of a sudden someone behind me said, "Hey get her up there and quit teasing her." It was Uncle James Auchiah, Francis Chanate, and Alford Gilbert. They were hunting rabbits. They were carrying what they kill. The fun was over. I got her up the hill, and we went home. That was a little fun time on a cold winter day.

Gma and Gpa are getting old, but they were still active. They like to work and did the best they could to take care of us. They didn't know how to speak a word of English, but somehow the white man understood the Indian. The white neighbors were real nice people. We play with them; they come to play with us, and we spend the night sometimes when we have the permission. Our neighbor, the lady Maces, gives us milk. Gpa help the white man butcher a beef or a hog, and they give him meat and pork. I mention before, Gpa was active at his age; he like to work. He built a barn for his horses, and he plants garden; he does a little artwork. He make large wooden spoons for all the neighbors ladies to stir their food. They were glad to have them.

Grandmother Kol-an-on-da-ma made most of her things such as cowhide bags. She will scrape all the hair off the hide after it dried. She soak the hide when hair is off, took it while it is soft. She used her awl to stitch the hide or bag with strips of buckskin. She fix it so it can be close or open. She can also storage other things, dried bote or dried plums. Gma was also art minded. She did art on her Kiowa calendar. She didn't do paint work; she used crayons for her colors. She went by seasons to tell what happens that made history. And I thought that she was the first person that had a Kiowa calendar, because people came to look at her calendar. She also named some people that was born during the season or month, and some people came to find their birth month. It was very interesting. She also had our birth months. My birth month was May. She had a drawing of a "colored" man that was hung in Anadarko. 1912 [1913]. The colored man attack a white lady. They hang him near the BIA office at Anadarko, where they were all camp there. Many other things she had in her calendar. Mr. George Hunt borrowed it and never return it to her. Later waiting for him to return it. He never did and she made another calendar. She also had a drawing of all the chiefs' tepee toward the end of her calendar. Later Mr. Hunt let Gma know that he turn it over to the [Smithsonian] at Washington DC. A copy of her second calendar is at the post museum near Lawton. And to my thinking, that's where the chief's te-pee are made from using the drawing of te-pee Grandma had on her calendar. The mini te-pee are also in Washington DC, and I think they were made from the patterns and drawings Gma had on her calendar.[41] Hope some of the descendants would ask for the calendar and keep it. Mr. Hunt just took it to look at it, and I would think that he took it on purpose, to copy for himself for his gain. He has some books out by Alice Marriott that mention some things Gma had in her calendar. And I have a copy of her second calendar.

A white lady came from Canada to work as a missionary among the Kiowa Indians. She left the comfort of her home to live among the Indians. She was a devoted young teenage when she came. Gma said she was eighteen [thirty-one] years of age, and she was good and kind to all our people. She taught them many things. She wanted a church built for the Indians. And, with the help of the mission board, a church was build. The men helped haul lumber. A dining hall was also build. The men stayed with the work until everything was finish. Esabell [Isabel] Crawford is the name of the young lady. She taught the women how to sew and make quilt. She lived among the Indians. She lived on Lucius Aitson's property.[42] She wanted to live in a te-pee, so they put up a te-pee for her. She drives a single buggy with one horse on Sunday mornings. Sometime she rides with Lucius Aitson. In her early days at Saddle Mountain, she came to the homes on Wednesdays for sewing meeting. She help the women cook and ate with them. She also help the women with food on Sunday at the church and help them in the camp. When someone is sick, or a child in the home, she visits and help. She spends some time in the home. She was a great woman. She was a wonderful Christian woman. Everybody love Miss Crawford and appreciate her very much. It is amazing how Miss Crawford taught the Indians to make them understand. They don't speak English, and they don't understand English. But they believed in the Lord and Jesus thru her teaching,

8. Saddle Mountain Baptist Church, after completion, circa 1906. Tongkeamha family photograph.

and their faith was strong. They were all faithful. Her mission work was a big success. The Kiowas responded and learned many good things. She turn them away from their idols. They believe the words of Bible and the living God and his son, Jesus. They compose many Indian hymns with the words from the Bible. My Gma Kol-an-on-da-ma compose four songs.

When her work was finish at Saddle Mountain, she went to Canada to live with her father. Her father was a minister. She never forgot her Indian people. She comes occasionally for Christmas and camp meetings, and she supported the church all the way with her gift of money. But I remember Miss Crawford. She went back to Canada, and she came to visit her Indian people. She come to Saddle Mountain when I was two years old. I saw her sat on the floor with the women to eat. Miss Crawford knew my mother also. I saw her several times. She comes during camp meetings. She promise her people that she would be buried with them when she passed away. She lived to be over ninety years old, and her body came to be buried at Saddle Mountain. The members had her funeral at the Saddle Mountain Church.[43] She loved her people very much, how they respond to her teaching. She was a beautiful lady. Her life was beautiful. On her headstone reads in these words (I come to dwell among my people). All members went to church; they did not stop when she passed away. She publish books telling about how she first came among the Kiowa people to work. The name of one of her books is Joyful Journey. How she lived in the te-pee, how she travel in her single buggy and horse. The Indian food she ate with them. How she help when they were sick. Isabel Crawford enjoyed her work at Saddle Mountain and stayed with the Indians after the church was complete. Miss Crawford did her work well. And she never forgot her people. Gma told us some of these things. Some. I don't quite remember, some of the things.

It was a habit for the members on Sunday mornings. They attend church every Sunday. We went to church more than anywhere else. So we look forward to Sundays. Gpa Ole-paugh hitch his horse to the wagon after breakfast on Sunday mornings, and Gma prepared her Sunday dinner and pack her dishes and food. We then get ready to dress in our Sunday clothes and help hitch the wagon, and all is ready. Off we go to church. And we all spend the day at the church. When the service are over, we all go home to our places. Saddle Mountain Church is a mile east of Gma and Gpa home. Some time I and my sister, Margaret, get anxious, and we walk against Gma's orders. Aunt Ruth and Uncle Sherman usually come over on Fridays and Saturdays to go to church. Also Aunt Hattie Spotted Horse and her family. All leave for home on Monday.

Every Sunday families travel on covered wagons to church faithfully. Wagon and buggies came from every direction, east, west, north, and south. Old Man Horse and family, the Stumbling Bears, and Frizzleheads came from east. The Auchiahs, Giemausaddles, and Gilberts came from west. The Tonemahs and Tanedoahs and the Carl Reids family came from north to church. The Aunkos and Akonedos from south. The Steven Kotays. The Horace Quetone family. Harry Hall and family. Eddie Long Horn and family. Felix Thompson family. They all have a big gathering on occasions. Thanksgiving, Easter, everyone bring dinner to church, and every Sundays families bring dinner. They have an all-day service. They camp for deacon conference. They have two-day conference. The host church prepare meals for the guest. Camp meetings were held at different churches. The Northern Baptist churches under the same mission board. The Red Stone Church west of Anadarko. The Rainy Mountain Church near Mountain View. The Deyo Mission and Post Oak Mission west of Lawton. North of Lawton was the Brown Church near Walters, Oklahoma. We camp at these churches annually for camp meeting. The Elk Creek Indian Mission has a campground west of Hobart, Oklahoma. The members of each church all camp. They haul their camp [equipment] in wagons. Everyone enjoy the camp and services.

There were ministers that came and went. The first pastor I remember was Mr. and Mrs. Rev. Parks. Next was Mr. and Mrs. Treat. Mr. and Mrs. Rev. Hicks. Mr. and Mrs. Jackson. Rev. Sherman Chaddleson.

Ioleta Hunt MacElhaney. Mr. and Mrs. Roy Saumpty. Uncle Sherman [Chaddleson] pastored several Indian Baptist churches. The Indian Baptist Church at Hobart. And at Saddle Mountain. The first church he pastored was the Apache Indian church east of Alden. Apache and Kiowas attend. The Red Bones, the Whites, the Tah's and A, the Frizzleheads, the Chainos, the Little Chiefs. The last church he was in charge of was the Red Stone Church, west of Anadarko. After he retired, they move to their home south of Mountain View. Near Sedan.

We look forward to going to Sunday school at Saddle Mountain Church. Mrs. Hicks was our Sunday school teacher. I learned many things from her. She said if we memorized the 94 Psalm, she would give a new Bible to the first one that memorize it. And I wanted the Bible very much and studied very hard, and I did get the Bible, and it was my prize possession. I was proud to have Bible. Going to church every Sunday and learning from our Sunday school teacher was very interesting. She taught us about the devil and etc. My sister, Margaret, got upset thinking that the devil would get us if we don't believe in God and be baptize. She cried to be baptize, so following Sunday she was baptize at Gpa Ole-paugh Spring. And she didn't cry anymore. I was baptize at the age of fifteen years [1927]. Most of the members were baptize at Gma Kol-an-on-da-ma Spring [Odlepaugh Springs]. Most of my relatives are Baptist.

During Christmas the families camp near the church. They start their camp a few days before Christmas. They camp all around the church on the east to the north and west to the south. The first Christmas camp I remember was in the early twenties. There were no beds or tables or chairs. Everything was on the ground. Gma chop tall red grass and bundle it together with tough twine. After she make several bundles, she lined them on the ground inside of the tent, one on the north side, west side, and south side and cover the bundles of grass with canvas to make pallet, and she put quilts and blankets over canvas, which make a soft pallet for bed to sleep on. They have an old cone-shape stove, which they call army stove that keep the tent warm, and Gma made a grill in front of the stove by digging a square-shape fireplace. She put the grill over the fireplace, and that where she cooks her meals. She also made a place for her dishes and cooking utensils with putting four small stakes in the ground and putting a lining on the top with some wood. And that's where she kept her dishes. She also put two long stakes in the ground and another wood across the two stakes on small poles with hooks, where she hang her water buckets. We all sit on the ground to eat. The tent was cozy and warm. Gma also line the inside of the tent with extra canvas, which makes it very warm. One Christmas it was so cold people chop ice to make camp. They brave the weather to do their duty as Christians. The Christmas camp is a joyful time. Everybody visit each other in camp. Inviting someone for a meal. They have few nites revival before the Christmas nite.

On Christmas Day everyone have the Christmas dinner in the large dining hall. When Christmas is over, some families stay in camp until after New Year's. They also celebrate the New Year. I enjoy these Christmas camps. Gma and Gpa Ole-paugh always have a tepee up. Aunt Hattie Spotted Horse, Aunt Ruth, and Uncle Sherman Chaddleson, they all camp close together. In the te-pee it is always cozy too. Gma also cook in the te-pee. She makes her coffee and cook meat in the fire. The members of the Saddle Mountain Church take everything to heart. They are always glad to celebrate Christ's birthday. They camp and enjoy the visiting and revival that began a few days before Christmas They make pledges; they pay money at Christmas. For many years the members upheld their church. They support it and was faithful. When Christmas camp is over, everybody get settle back to their homes.

We had many good times in our young days. I love to listen to the stories Gpa tells us. He also like to sing. Gma also like to sing. I remember some of the old songs, especially old church hymns. I don't remember some of the stories that Gma and Gpa told us, and I do remember some of the Sane-day stories and others. I enjoy the nite when Gpa tells us stories. And some nite he would take his pipe and tobacco out of a special bag that Gma made for him and smoke.

He seemed to be thinking or concentrating of things of long ago; he would sit for a long time as he smoke his pipe. He made the pipe himself. Gma and Gpa had several Indian relics and costumes. They also had a painted te-pee. Gma saved the te-pee. In 1930 tornado destroyed Gma's home, and everything went with it.[44] Gma made all their costumes.

My grandpa and them, they went to Dietrich's Lake, and they were still involved in dancing. But, as far as worshipping other [religions], whatever, I didn't see them do that. They didn't. They just went to the powwows, and they say that these are old traditions. The Kiowas, they go to powwows, and it doesn't mean anything about worshipping anything at the powwows. But they go. And I remember them camping over there at Dietrich's Lake, and we were still small yet. I and my sister. And whenever they camped they put up a te-pee. Some of the Kiowas, they put up te-pees. Of course, they had te-pees and tents, so that's what they did when they camped. And I think they camped about twice, that I remember. And then maybe that was moved to Craterville then. You have to travel in a wagon to Craterville. And they also put up their tent over there; it was in the early twenties, when Dietrich's Lake. Tom Dietrich was the captive, captive by the Comanche tribe. And he seemed to treat the Comanches special; he has a certain place for them to camp on that south end. Tom can really speak Comanche.[45]

And we go up there, and we'd camp. Slept on the ground, spread canvas out, slept right on the ground. Spread canvas out, cook out in the open campfire. I guess it kind of remind him of the old ways that the parents, the grandparents, [lived]. But they get so used to that kind of living that they enjoyed it. And they was still having powwows, but they didn't have no benches, no tables, just open on the ground. They don't have no benefit; they don't have no way of raising funds. They always come together and then butcher a beef, and they pass the meat. And whatever they got, they just got along with it. They never raised no benefit to put a powwow on. They never did that; they just stayed, camped until it's over.[46]

About four days, but they camp ahead, a few days before, and just prepare the camp for their powwow. And Dietrich said he'd give a beef to each tribe, and he's let them chase it, with a bow and arrow, kill it and butcher it. I don't know how often he did that. But things weren't too high in those days, so I don't know how much cattle were worth, but he gave it. And then it was moved to Craterville Park. That Frank Rush, he's the one that was the sponsor. And he sponsored it like Dietrich's Lake did. I don't know what happen to Tom Dietrich. But he still lived there after that. And he gives buffalos, that Frank Rush. He give buffalo to butcher and distribute the meat. So that was carried on for several years. I think it was longer than the Dietrich's. And the army bought that land, so they had to close it. Government land.[47]

They parade in their costumes at Craterville Park near Eagle Park during the early twenties. They have a big celebration annually. Kiowa, Comanche, [Plains] Apache tribes all camp. That's where the Indian fair originate. The sponsor was Mr. Frank Rush. Programs are horse racing, parade powwow, and woman stick games. Women kickball games compete with tribe. Baseball game and lady basketball game. Kiowa girls compete with Comanche girls. Gma and Gpa usually camp to take part in the parade and powwow. It was always good to be there. Gma and Gpa take part in the Indian rituals once a year at the Lone Bear dance ground, where they celebrate the Fourth of July. They have a big camp and four days powwows. They gourd dance and war dance, and the other place they go is at Craterville Park, where they have the Indian fair every year. Aunt Hattie Spotted Horse helps them when they camp.

And then the Kiowas moved to Anadarko. The exposition. When they had it at Craterville, that's when the Indians learned how to plant gardens and the women learned how to can fruit and vegetables. And then they put those things up for exhibits; they give them prize for it. They used to do that; they had prizes for canned goods. They even had some of them bring their horses to exhibit, show. Some of them had nice-looking horses. And they'd get prize for it, poultry too, chickens. They had all that, everything. Cows, a few people owned cows. My in-laws, Weiser's folks, they had had cows. One time the old man, he won a sow with pigs. They said, whoever had the best garden. They had a lot of programs. The BIA encouraged the Indians how to build up, be self-supporting. And they put out some advertisement saying whoever had the garden will get a sow with pigs.[48]

As time and years go by, I know Gpa and Gma is getting very old. As I have mention, we lived with them, and sometime I would stay with Aunt Hattie Spotted Horse. And we also stay at Aunt Lizzie's home. It is always hard to accept death in the family. Gpa was very old, and his health was failing. He was sick only a few months and passed away in 1923. We were still living with them, and we all felt the loss. Gma grief for a long time. I cry when she cried. My aunts take care of her; they all take turns taking care of her. Grandpa was a loving person, concern for his daughters and grandchildren. He was kind; he never raise his voice at us, never lifted hand to strike anyone. We all loved him. He taught us many good things. Him and Lucius Aitson are half brothers. Same mother but different fathers. Lucius is the son of Mo-keen, a Mexican captive. Mo-keen was captured by the Kiowas. He was a teenage boy herding sheep when he was captured.[49] Lucius was the first interpreter for Esabell [Isabell] Crawford. Richard Aitson is the son of Lucius Aitson. Lucius passed away before his father, Mo-keen. Grandpa Ole-paugh let Mo-keen live with us now and then. Mo-keen drives a single buggy. He was a faithful member of Saddle Mountain Church. He never miss a Sunday. As time and years went by, we lived with Gma. She was also getting very old. And we some stay with Aunt Lizzie and her husband. I can't recall the year when Gma Susie's home was hit by lightning and burn down. I was very sad for the family, a great loss. Aunt Lizzie let her brothers live with her at Saddle Mountain.

I and sister Margaret became teenage. I met the man I married at Saddle Mountain Church, Weiser Tongkeamha. His folks started to church the year 1926. His older brother, Frank Tongkeamha, passed away in 1925. I and Weiser got married July 10, 1928. We lived with his folks near Cache Creek. His brother Frank T had one daughter. Frank's wife passed away when his daughter Peggy was a few months old. Weiser's parents raise her. She was three years old when I came to live with them. My sister, Margaret, got married to Billy High Methvin.[50] They lived with Billy's grandfather Sidney High. Our father, Fremont, married Minnie Aitson. Minnie was married twice before. First husband was Amos Aitson, son of Lucius Aitson. He passed away, and she married his brother L[ucius B.] Aitson. After several years he also passed away. And Dad married her. Had another tragedy in his family. Gma Kol-an-on-da-ma's home was destroyed by a tornado May 22, 1930. No one was home at the time. Gpa Oyebi came to visit us occasionally. He was the same good grandfather. He never raise his voice to anyone. I can proudly say my grandparents on both sides of family are the best, kind, and loving grandfathers. Gpa Oyebi was also getting very old. I appreciate my grandparents on both side of family.

Gma Kol-an-on-da-ma went blind; she was too old, and nothing could be done for her blindness. I know Gma was very lonely since Gpa left us. She was active until she went blind. She stayed with us now and then when I got married. She lived with Aunt Ruth and Uncle Sherman when tornado destroyed her home. Grandma Kol-an-on-da-ma passed away the year [1934]. I love my grandparents very much, and I want to do so much for them if they had live when I got married.

Brother Bruce never got married. He was in failing health for several months. He came to our place and stay on for days. He wasn't doing so well. The doctor advise Bruce to be in the hospital at Talehina [Talihina].[51] Dad took him, and he was there for four months. One day we received the sad news that Bruce had terminal tuberculosis, and there was nothing they could do for him. The doctor mention that if we want him at home they would arrange to bring him home. So we had him at Aunt Lizzie's place, where Dad and Minnie were living. Bruce became bedfast for three month, and he passed away May 1, 1936. The hurt was a great loss for us. We love our brother very much. When he was sick, Dad did all he could for him. He wanted things that Dad got for him. He enjoyed them a while and get tired of them. We try to give him a good day every day. We were there with him; we talk to him and cheer him up. But there is a time for each one of us that we would depart from this world. Dad grief so much he became sick and did not care to get well. Three months after Bruce passed away, father passed away August 3, 1936. He did not get to move in their new home. He was in the hospital for two weeks in July and came home to Gpa Oyebi's home near Fort Cobb and passed away there. Somehow we lived through these sadness.

Bruce was a nice quiet boy; he like sports. Those that knew him said he was a nice-looking young man. He had several friends. I and my sister, Margaret, was proud of our brother. Our other brother is Herman Lee Oyebi, our half brother. Evelyn Oyebi Chalepah is our half sister. Brother Herman was also a good-looking young man.

I and my husband had twelve children, seven girls and five boys. Our oldest daughter, Carene, passed away 1929, age one and a half. Second daughter passed away age [one] year. Her name is Shirley Jean Tongkeamha. I raise five girls and five boys. Oldest son Wallace, Clifton, Lavena, Melissa, Raymond, James, Bruce, Becky, Prenella, and Lisa Tongkeamha. My sister Margaret and Billy Methvin had five boys and four girls. Our half sister, Evelyn Apayyat Chalepah, married Alfred Chalepah. They had six girls and seven boys. Our half brother, Herman Lee Apayyat, did not have any children; also our oldest, Bruce Kinney Apayyat, did not have any children.

When Aunt Lizzie's first husband, Thomas, passed away, she married George Silver Horn. They have one daughter, Lauretta Ruth S. Horn. Minnie move in her new house. Her son and his wife lived with her. Franklin and Amy Aitson and their children. Grandpa Oyebi's wife passed away, and he lived with Aunt Lizzie again. Uncle Winston was married to Hattie Tay-kune, and they lived near Hog Creek. Before Gpa Oyebi lived with Aunt Lizzie, Uncle Tom and Gpa lived near Fort Cobb, where Gpa lived with his wife. Uncle Tom got married to Carrie Poor Buffalo, and they moved to the old home place, where we all used to live before Gma Susie [died]. Gpa Oyebi had three-room house build on the old home place. Aunt Lizzie and husband live there awhile, until Uncle Tom got married. She move to Cyril on her allotment, and she took care of Gpa Oyebi there. [He passed away in 1942.]

# 2  Raymond Tongkeamha's Memoirs

## Overview

Born on June 15, 1942, Raymond Tongkeamha can recall, as his ear-
liest memories, his parents; Grandma Fannie; older siblings Wallace,
Clifton, Lavena, and Melissa; and nephew Frank (b. 1938)—son of
Reuben Stumbling Bear (1915–94) and Peggy Tongkeamha (1922–
94), the daughter of Weiser's deceased brother, Frank. Raymond's
other childhood playmate was Herman Lee Methvin (1941–94), the
son of Henrietta's sister, Margaret. Though reckoned as first cousins,
they are brothers according to Kiowa custom.[1] No different than
other Native Americans, Raymond and his companions acquired
childhood nicknames. Frank was dubbed "Jughead," though Clifton, not surprisingly, called him "Doghead." Long-legged Herman
Lee earned the moniker "Daddy Long Legs," which later became
"Spider," then shortened to "Spi." Roderick Gwoompi (1940–2009),
Raymond's nephew through his mother, was called "Sambo" in his
youth and "Smokey" in adulthood. In his poem "Sobriquet" Ray
Doyah (2003, 27–28) humorously portrays Kiowa boys learning
one another's given name the first day of school. Doyah—a member

of Raymond's age cohort—identifies the nicknames of classmates: Pig, Worm, Crazy, Sluggo, Squint, Strawberry, Donkey, Hess, Tonk [Raymond], Chow Boy, Dawes, Sambo, Minnow, Lease Man, June Bug, Joe Fish, Spider, Herb, Fino, Charley Bugs, Whale, Cook, Booty, and Round Brown. When the teacher recites the first-grade roster, the children snicker upon learning everyone's true identity—James, George, Joseph, William, and so on.

The old homestead thirteen and a half miles south of Carnegie is situated along the upper reaches of East Cache Creek. West of the creek, a concrete slab—the front porch—discernable through the underbrush, signifies where the house once stood. Gone are the barn, garden, peach orchard, dance grounds, and ball field across the creek. The only visible sign of human habitation is a tent, fire pit, and other accoutrements of Raymond's encampment, where he finds occasional respite from society. Otherwise it's difficult imagining a thriving farm with cattle, horses, chickens, dogs, garden, and outbuildings. Only memories remain.

By the mid-twentieth century, Christianity rapidly spread throughout Kiowa country, despite the scarcity of community-based mission churches, which necessitated meeting in people's homes. "Cottage prayer meetings" were popular around the time Henrietta and Weiser were married, though the Tongkeamha allotment was only ten miles away from Saddle Mountain Church. Their strong commitment to the mission church is evident in the KCA Intertribal Cemetery—east of where the church and dining hall once stood—where several generations of Tongkeamhas rest in the extended family plot. By the early 1960s outmigration from the surrounding countryside led to the decline of the church, and in November 1963 the church closed and the buildings were sold and moved sixteen miles southwest to Eagle Park; thirty years later services resumed in a donated house trailer south of the cemetery (Kracht 2018, 215–16, 152–53, 202–3). A quarter century later loss of a pastor, low attendance, and untenable upkeep for Raymond—the sole caretaker—contributed to discontinuing services and closing the church in September 2019. Until

9. Raymond Tongkeamha on the front porch of his old homestead, May 2018. Photograph by Benjamin Kracht.

then Raymond served as lay pastor. Old photographs on the walls—Isabel Crawford, charter members, Odlepaugh, Kiowa Jim, Weiser, Henrietta, Raymond, and his siblings and relatives at gatherings and Christmas encampments—are no longer there; the abandoned mobile home awaits its fate.[2]

When not in school, Henrietta spent much of her childhood and adolescence close to home, working and occasionally traveling to neighboring towns with her grandparents, whereas Raymond left frequently and wandered farther. Most of Henrietta's stories are about life with her grandparents, and she tells few personal tales, whereas Raymond shares engaging stories of his adventures and exploits. Henrietta wrote about friendly relationships with non-Indian neighbors, but Raymond's accounts suggest that amicable relations diminish as one gets closer to the towns, especially Carnegie. Kiowa oral traditions and personal experiences verify that racism exists in Carnegie, Anadarko, and other towns in southwestern Oklahoma.

Carnegie, an agricultural community on the Chicago, Rock Island and Pacific Railroad line, reached its zenith before the Great Depression, which caused some outmigration. By midcentury the town of 1,700 residents still boasted grocery stores, gas stations, garages, hardware stores, hotels, beer joints, automobile dealerships, cafés, ice cream parlors, movie theaters, cotton gins, and an ice plant. Since then the rail line has been abandoned and the tracks removed. Merchants benefiting from the 1970s oil boom went out of business in the 1980s. Driving through town today, one can espy the empty shells of Dixie Store, Kelley's Grocery, and other long-abandoned buildings, whereas the Liberty Theatre is still operating. The former ice plant now houses a small grocery store. The open field behind Kelley's makes it difficult to imagine Indians watering their horses and visiting there on Saturdays.

From no indoor plumbing or electricity to radios, televisions, and big-box stores, Raymond has witnessed many transformations in his life. Leaving home in the early 1960s, he encountered the world beyond southwestern Oklahoma through military service and jobs in Oklahoma City, Dallas, and elsewhere before returning home several decades ago. Today he often seeks solace from the outside world at the old homestead along East Cache Creek, where he reminisces about friends and relatives from the past. His stories are embedded in the landscape, as are the songs emanating from the old dance grounds. There he anticipates reuniting with the ancestors waiting for him on the other side.

## Editing

Raymond's narrative needed little editing. Punctuation was inserted or deleted, but grammar and slang remain unaltered to preserve his storytelling voice, especially in humorous stories. Some spellings and abbreviations were kept: "U," "N," "lil," "kno," "kinda," "sorta," "ur," "outta," "tho," "rite," "nuff," "ole," "shor," "hatchin," "havin," "lol," and " ☺"; whereas "yrs," "Y," and "&" were changed to "years" and "and." On rare occasions spellings and capitalization were adjusted.

Occasional box brackets insert missing words, dates, and translations. Endnotes provide ethnographic details and backstories. Otherwise, changes were unnecessary.

## May 2018 Narrative

I am going to go back in the time of my life that I can best remember. When I was about four or five years of age to the present time. I'm seventy-four years old now [2016], tho sometimes I feel much younger. Born at Kiowa Indian Hospital, Lawton, Oklahoma, June 15, 1942. Incidentally, my dad, Weiser Tongkeamha, and I have the same birthday.

I'm not a writer per se, but I'm a printer by trade. I feel the need to leave something about me to whomever is interested. Who or what I'm about. Hope I don't leave too many things out. I will cover as much as I can. Dad, Weiser, Mom, Henrietta Apayyat Tongkeamha, Grandma, Fannie Tah-po-mah Tongkeamha (Dad's mom), were the main people in my life at my early age.

I remember being around Grandma mostly. She died in 1950. I remember that day. She had a lil room on the southwest side of our house. She was sick for some time. Dad was in her room that day sitting with her. I think I felt that something wasn't good that day. She'd been in Shawnee Sanitarium for some time, and we'd go see her. I didn't kno what was wrong, as I was too young to understand. One day Dad said that they (hospital) had found a spot on her lung. Well, I sure didn't kno what that meant then. Found out later that she had TB. After a while they just brought her home to her lil room.

People would come and sit with her. Don't think Dad ever left her side. One day Dad came rushing out of her room, wringing his hands and crying, talking in Kiowa mostly to himself, saying, "Mom has gone on," over N over. I myself was pretty bewildered. I couldn't, wouldn't, or did not want to believe what just happened. Nephew Jughead [Frank Tongkeamha] was sitting on this high chair hanging his head and crying. Guess I was just crushed, as Grandma and I were really close. We were always together seemed like. She made me pretty aw-dae [spoiled]. Anyway, there was this old lady that was her close friend and spent a lot of time with her was there. Hawley or Holly was her name. Sister Melissa said that the lady was a Guoladdle. Well, this old lady really did cry hard. Scared me the way she cried and for so long. Shaking, convulsing. She sure thought a lot of Grandma. I was eight years old then, but it seemed like we spent a lot of years together. Her wake and funeral was the "old way." Sitting up all nite at the house. Prayers, Kiowa hymns. I wondered what was going on. But what did I know about anything at that time. But sometimes I'd wish things should have stayed that way. All I needed then was Grandma. Talk about aw-dae.

I was so glad when the idea of getting a headstone for Grandma at Saddle Mountain came about. All these years she didn't have one. I suggested it to my sisters and Jughead that we should pitch in and get her one. So we got her one, and I sure enjoy cleaning her grave and rest of my family. I get to visit with them yet. Wish we had one for Grandpa, James "Kiowa Jim" Tongkeamha. He had gone on by the time I was born. Sure wish I had got to know him. Heard many good stories about him tho, from Dad and others that saw or knew him. From other tribes also. So I have a good mental picture of him.

Dad had a baseball diamond across the creek. I remember Dad playing and the Horse and Geionty brothers on Dad's team. Chester, David, Stanley Horse; Robert, George, Wilbur, and Warren Geionty brothers. I sure admired them. U could drive down and thru the creek to get to the ball field. It was rite across creek to the right in the corner of pasture. I still can imagine the Model T's and Model A's driving across and parking and honking. They really honked when someone hit a home run. They were all good ballplayers. If u seen them years later u wouldn't think they played or were good, but they were. George Chaino, John Chaino, Fritz Kauley, Buster Tsontakoy, to name a few.

About a hundred yards north of home plate was a gate to the field. By the gate was some plum bushes. That's where Grandma had our "stadium seat," her blanket on the ground, plums right behind us, plus her always handy (aye-sahn) snacks. Dried apricots, raisins, pounded dried meat mixed with bone marrow, and possum grapes. Yum! Also close by was our water well with its icy cold and delicious-tasting water. That water was cold. Some old people that are still around still ask if that well is still there. All there is now is a small indentation where it used to be. Floods covered it up. We had a frame over it with a grooved pulley for the rope with a bucket on the end. Drop the bucket down the water and pull it up. There seemed to be a science to getting that bucket to tip over down there to fill with water. I would get frustrated, especially if Clifton or Jughead were around, as they would watch me trying to get water in that bucket. Just laugh at me. "Boy that guy!" "Maw-bahn" [Goofy]. But I finally got the hang of it. Then carry it down across the creek, up the hill and to the house. About a hundred yards. Sometimes two buckets. Boy! Help? Huh-unh. I mean, sometimes, maybe. Don't kno if Grandma understood the game. But we sure enjoyed ourselves. I kinda think she knew something of the game. Chester Horse was a pretty good pitcher.[3] I could hear Grandma hollerin, "C'mon Chesta Boy!" Warren Geionty played center field, and he was a short guy whose ears stood out and his chest also. He was good and fast. They called him "Mighty Mouse."

Dad said Grandpa had a dance ground the same place. Wish I coulda seen it then. O-ho-mah, Ton-kong-g'yah [Black Leggings], and other dances; some that they don't do anymore. Grandma was always sewing or bead working. She had her hide bag with all her stuff in it. Elk horn for scraping, awl, sinew for thread, and other hides around. I'd put a piece of hide on and go to the bush in front yard to wait for Lavena and Melissa to come from school. Sh-eh, I didn't even scare them, but Grandma would be hollering about "where the hides at."

Some days Grandma would start moving around like she's getting ready to do something. Tie her shawl on, so I knew we were going somewhere, as she'd grab a gunny sack and her stick. Across the creek we'd go. To the pasture. There was a big prairie-dog town there.

She'd sing that prairie-dog song to them. She was after "k'awn-k'ee," box turtle terrapin. She'd point them out to me with her stick. "Ayndae," "this one." I'd pick it up to put in her sack, but it would pee on me, and I wasn't too "on" about that, but she got a "charge" out a that. Sometimes she'd stop and look around, tho not at the ground. I would wonder about that. Then she'd say, "oo-gaw," "over there." I didn't see anything, but I'd pick up different plants until she'd say "ayn-haw-dae" (that's it). "Ah-sayhn-ohn." "Indian perfume." She sure did know her plants, as that's what she used when she "doctored." Finally, we made it home with our catch or meal.

We had a cast-iron wood-burning kitchen stove, which she would fire up. Then she'd dump those turtles into the oven alive. Course when that oven started heating up, you could hear them moving around. After a while they really started moving around and making a scratching noise. A little later you could hear, "p'sssh'!" Bust open. Smelled meat. They're done. Eat 'em outta the shell. It's A-B-C-delicious. Grandma would be singing that '49 turtle song: Ahn-ah-hay-maw, k'awn-kee-maut-ha-sayh, maw-gyah-hayn-p'ehn-p'ong-gyah-aye-yah-hay-yeah![4] South of the house, quarter mile was a peach orchard. Grandma would pick only the green ones. She would fry these. I wondered at that. But she dried them. Good tho. One time I saw Grandma out back of the house, standing with her back to the tree, moving. I asked Dad what she was doing. He said, "Oh, she's scratching her back." Scratching tree. Seen cows do that.

Back then those winter nites were cold. Seemed like that north room was the coldest. We had a rectangular cast-iron woodstove in the front room. Grandma had this oval-shaped almost-flat smooth rock she would heat up, then wrap it in a cloth, which she placed under the covers at the foot of the bed. I slept with her. Well, u put ur feet on that rock, and it sure warmed u up. Sometimes we'd push the other's feet off that rock. Hoggin it. Have our lil foot fight. Think she liked to fight with me. We'd be sitting on the blanket on the ground at the ballgame or wherever else we'd sit together. She'd be quiet, but after a while she'd slightly elbow me. Then do it again, until I'd get mad and say something. She'd slowly turn her head to me, and I'd see her give me a slow slight grin. I'd be mad at her but guess she liked that. Then she'd say, "Non-do-ay saw hn-dae-aw-maw" (Why you get mad?). Summers were also pretty hot. No air conditioner or electricity. We had what was called an "icebox." A wooden cabinet like thing with sections in it for food, etc., and a lil larger space for a fifty-pound block of ice from town. It had thick walls with tin lining. Well, one day I figured it was hotter than usual, so what I do. I opened the door to it where the ice would be put. (There was no ice in there in some time.) Anyway, I got in there and sat down. Here come Grandma and seen me in there. She said, "Junior Boy, what u do in the icebox?" Heard Lavena crackin up. I associated it with being cool even tho there hasn't been any ice in it for some time. Coolin my heels, gotta think positive.

Our nephew, Frank Tongkeamha, better known to us as "Jughead," was always into things. Always catching it. He was about four years older than me. His mother was Peggy Estelline Tongkeamha, whose dad was Frank Tongkeamha: Dad's older brother who passed on before I came along. He would pick on Lavena at times. He challenged her one day, saying she couldn't "flop" me. Boy she got mad and got hold of him and "flopped" him. Made the dust fly. He was about to cry and give a forced brave grin, but he said, "Bet you can't do it again." But she did. Mawn-sape iti "imp."

In front of the house were some "ae't-t'ah-pohl" trees (locust trees). Lotta shade. Under those trees Grandma had her "tso-t'sain" (board bed) and woodwork bench. She'd sit with her friend, Holly Guoladdle, sewing and visiting. Jughead was running around with some kids, playing in his cutoff pants and down-at-the-heel cowboy boots. The sides of his boot heel were so wore down it looked like he was running on the sides of his ankles. Guess Grandma got tired of seeing him run and walk like that. She hollered at him, "Jaw-Head, aim-ahn' zame-t'ay" (Come here, shame on you). She got his boots off and knocked the heels off with her hatchet. Well, that "pit stop" fixed him up. He took off running flat out and straight. Dad would say, "That fixed his lil red wagon."

We had a lil wheeled wagon we'd push or drag each around with. A slope ran down to the creek in front of our sidewalk and driveway. Well, Jughead would tell me to get in that wagon. He'd pad me up with some old clothes from the barn. Even some kind of helmet. Bucket? He thought of my safety. Then he'd push me toward the slope toward the creek. I'd guide it with the handle folded back. He shoved me down that hill to the creek. I never did have a soft landing, or he'd pull the wagon by the handle and make a really sharp turn. Course I'd flip out, dust flying, me crying. He'd say, "What chu cry'n for. Germans don't cry." Well, I wasn't no German!

We had a dugout cellar with granite rock fitted together for walls. Board and tin roof. I wonder now how we all fit in there. A bad storm was coming up and, as usual, Mom was hollerin at us to get in the cellar. But Grandma was still standing out there talking to it. She had her palm of her hand held out and straight vertical. I asked Dad, "What she was doing?" He said she was telling it (storm) to split and go around us. Don't know if it worked, but she'd do that with a knife or hatchet. I sure hated to go to the cellar, but we all had to. Get up when ur sleeping good, go out, and get wet and muddy. Mom said their house at Saddle Mountain blew away in a tornado. Her and her Grandma Ah-nan-thay [Kol-an-on-da-mah] and Grandpa Odlepaugh came out next day, and everything was gone. So she had a reason, I guess.[5]

Me? Well, I was a pretty quiet kid. Didn't like to say too much. Like I said, I was mostly around Grandma. I heard and observed a lot but didn't comment very much. Pretty self-conscious. I'd rather go fishing or hunting alone, as I would have better luck without all the noise others would make. When visitors would come over, they'd make comments about their kids. Mom would say, "Ayn-dae t'ohn-hay'n-daw." Meant me, "I don't talk." Or no talk. Easily embarrassed. Feelings easily hurt. Pretty shy guy. I am sure I had some strong traits tho. I just tried to stay outta the way. Dad said I was stubborn as a mule. I remember one time they came back from town, and we'd run out to meet them to see if they bought anything for us kids. Well, they got their toys or candy. But me? There was a funny book then that had a picture of a billy goat on the cover with coveralls on, eating a tin can. Know what? That comic book was called "Raymond the Goat." Think I threw that book down and ran to the creek. I did not think that was funny. Actually, didn't like my name after that. Thought I was so "maw-bahn." Maybe somebody got a kick outta that.

I was painfully bashful. Not quite an outsider though. I enjoyed being in the woods. I'd quietly sit there and listen or watch the animals come out. You hear about owls turning their heads completely around? Looks like it. This owl would always be on the same tree, rite down the creek. He'd always be looking out of his hole in the tree at me. He was sitting on a limb one day, and [I] figured I'd check his head turn out. So I walked round and round that tree, but his eyes were always on me. I thought, well, I'm gonna keep walkin around that tree 'til his head twists off. Well it didn't. You couldn't tell it but when that owl's head gets almost to a 360 degree turn, it spins back the other way so fast you couldn't hardly tell it. Found him out. Lil saw-pole [owl] almost fooled me. Ehn-haw!

Dad didn't believe me when I told him there were minks and muskrats down there. I even captured three or four minks alive one time. I made a cage out of door screen. We went to town one day, and when we got back I checked the cage, and it was torn open. They were long gone. Wallace said their momma came after them, as they were babies about seven inches long. I wondered what brother Wallace said. I thought, well, there goes Mom's mink coat! Buh!

One time I shot a squirrel that had babies in her nest. I heard them and felt bad. I climbed up and got them and took them home. They were real little and blind. Sisters Becky and Prenella had these lil plastic doll bottles for their dolls. Well, I put some milk in those lil bottles and, you know, those lil squirrels took rite to them. Got to where they'd stand up on their hind legs and hold the bottle. I put them in a dresser drawer and put a nite lite in there to keep them warm. Mom would hear their lil chirping and holler at me that my babies were crying and to feed them. They stayed in the trees outside for a long time. Finally left. Wallace scolded me about hunting in the springtime because that's when animals had young ones. Good lesson. Think Mom would wonder what I had, no tellin. Oh man, another time I was out in the creek when I spied this big ole owl sitting in a thorn bush tree. Just for the heck of it I whipped a rock at him and conked him out. I don't know why but decided to take him home.

Oh yeah, my brother Herman Lee (Spi) Methvin was with me. He wasn't too "on" with me taking that owl home.[6] It was windy that day, and I had a hard time staying on the ground with that owl flapping and that wind trying to lift it and me. Scared him. Getting home, I didn't really know what to do with it. In a room corner in the north room, Mom had a closet. A wooden rod was placed across that corner with a sliding curtain. Hangs her coats there. Yep, that's where I tied that saw-pole. Temporarily, supposedly. Well I forgot all about it until they got home. As usual, she went in there, pulled back the curtain to hang her coat. Thought I heard a mountain lion screaming in there and hollerin some not too good Kiowa words! Guess that thing was sitting there looking at her and man, oh man. My name was echoing around that house, "Get that thing outta here!" Dad 'bout took me apart! What was I thinking anyway? Leave it to me. I was walking thru the creek one day kinda hunting, but not really. I spied a big squirrel nest in a tree. Something was sitting in it that looked like a bobcat. I shot it between the eyes, and it tumbled out. It was another great horned owl. For whatever reason I climbed the tree just to see what was in the nest. Ha, there were three owl eggs in it. Here I go. I took them home with me.

I got a towel and wrapped those eggs in it and put them in a dresser drawer. Then I put a small nite light in there. Incubator? I guess. One day I got a lil awl-law-gyah ($) and headed to wherever I go. Rats, I forgot all about those eggs. They probably were getting close to hatchin or whatever. Anyway, upon finally returning home, I went to check on those eggs. Huh! They were gone. Maw-bahn, I should have known better, but I asked Mom. Thinking I had them hid. "Mom, have you seen those things?" "Those things?! I throwed them out!" "You quit bringing those things around!" Anyway. Okay, there went my experiment. These are just some of the things that went on. Probably too many to mention. The country was my world to me then and still is. "You can take the boy from the country, but you can't take the country from the boy."

I think it was before I started school, at Alden; I reckon I might fantasized a bit. Mom would be sewing on her foot-petal Singer sewing machine. I would be "big game" hunting down the creek. I don't know how I came up with the names of those animals. Anyway, when I came in Mom would ask me where I been or doing. I'd say hunting. She ask me did I get anything? Just like that, I'd say, yeah. What did you get, she'd say. Well, I shot some lions, tigers, elephants, etc. Then she'd ask me, where are they? Did you bring them? Well, I told her, you know, thems things is big, and I couldn't carry them, so I left them. She told me I should a brought them. I said I would next time. "You jes wait!" They're probably still out there. And leprechauns? I heard about them somehow. I'd sneak down the creek and lay down on my stomach for a long time watching. I was gonna catch me one. But I think they always just hide and watch me 'til I get tired and leave. Next time I'd come from another direction, but those guys are pretty smart, I guess. A big muskrat would try to fool me, but I caught on to him. First time I ever seen one down there. Wondered what was making that big splashing noise. I described it to Wallace, and he told me what it was. Biggest mouse I ever seen.

Dad taught me a lot about the outdoors, but it was Wallace who taught me the finer things. I learned a lot on my own also. I had patience then. I used to wonder how Wallace would spot something when I couldn't. I soon found out how to do that. He showed me how to handle a rifle and shoot, and I better not miss. Dad was a pretty good shot. If you didn't hit a squirrel or rabbit in the head first shot, he'd look at you like you were pretty low-life. Woe to you if you hit one in the stomach. When hit in the stomach, squirrel or rabbit would make it to a hole and a slow agonizing death, Wallace would say. Lead poisoning. He'd make you climb that tree to get that squirrel outta that hole or nest. Same for other game. Don't leave them to die like that.

Remembering back, we literally lived off the land. Dad had a big garden north side of the barn. Lots of potatoes, corn, green beans, cucumbers, radishes, onions, watermelons. Tending that garden was hard work. Planting, watering, which we carried from the creek, which was about seventy yards away. Pulling weeds, hoeing, etc. Then digging those potatoes up. You better not cut one potato while digging them. We had so many, we'd store them in the barn granary. Mom would can the green beans, which we had to snap after picking them. Smaller cucumbers she'd pickle in the mason jars. Corn we'd "husk" by hand. Rough. We had several wild plum bushes across the creek in that pasture. They were good size and juicy good. Also wild possum grapes in the creek. North up the creek was a bigger spring, which we called "the spring." There's a lot of pecan trees but by the spring was kinda of a pecan grove. We'd all go down there, rake the dead leaves away from the trees, and Dad would cut a green branch about the size of a baseball bat and fling it up among the limbs. Pecans showered down. Or if one of us could, we'd climb up and grab limbs or jump on them to shake pecans loose. I would wonder how could Dad throw that club far up there. Those trees are tall. Not much foothold to climb them. I tried to throw that club up there one time but sh-eh, forget it. Crawl around picking up pecans all day. Mom right in there with us. A gunnysack full would weigh about a hundred pounds. Do good to get three sacks full. Seemed like pecans were selling like eighteen to twenty-seven cents a pound then. But Dad would wait until he had a chance to go to Lawton to sell his because of the higher price. Carnegie was too cheap. In the long cold winters, we had wild-plum jam and biscuits, plus homemade candy. Rabbits, squirrel, fish, and garden foods. Guess we were "kaw-awn" (poor), but we wouldn't have known that. Far as we knew, we were A-okay. I remember one time, on a day before Thanksgiving, I overheard Mom and Dad talking about not going to have much for Thanksgiving dinner. It was snowing real hard that day when I seen Dad walk toward the highway across the wheat field with a gunnysack full of something. Going to pawn or sell something so we'd have something for Thanksgiving.

Well, I didn't know how our food situation was but figured it wasn't too good. So I took the .22 rifle down; there was only about twelve shells left. Shells were precious to us, so we better not waste any. I went out early toward Tracey's Ranch south thru the creek. I had to make every shot count and I did. You know, we had about the best Thanksgiving I know of. I had a deer and two wild turkeys, plus squirrel and rabbit. Dad also brought something from town and we feasted. He sure was surprised to see what I brought in. Mom told me I should give the other turkey to Uncle and Aunt Jennie Horse, so I did that. Praise the Lord for providing. Now this was kinda funny to Dad, I guess. I told him I knew I hit one turkey in the head, but why was another one flopping around. I told him I thought it was "puttin on." He cracked up. Turns out I got both of them with one shot. No witness that time, but that's what happened. I made other shots that you wouldn't believe, and other times I had witnesses. Wallace would look at me, grin a lil, and shake his head. No comment, James would say something, but he seen it. I used to almost beg Mom or Dad to buy me a BB gun. Even leave lil notes in the car when they went to town. No! Not this time. But I didn't give up. Maybe they couldn't afford it, but I just thought they always had money. Grandma too. One Saturday, lo and behold, Dad handed me a brand-new, single-shot BB gun. You had to break it open to cock it, then drop a BB down the barrel. I was in "tall cotton." Didn't matter what kind. I had a BB gun. I was ready for a safari. Ha, I found out that if I put a BB down the barrel to shoot, better keep the barrel at least level, not pointed down as the BB would roll out. Many an elephant lived on because I forgot that!

Woo! Christmas at Saddle Mountain Church. Dad would put up our camp there for about a week and a half. We'd have a school Christmas break through New Year's. Five nites before Christmas there would be a church service. Lotsa people, camps, kids. We'd have to attend, or else. There'd be different preachers there. Boy, those old people can pray, give testimony, and sing forever. It would be just packed. Carolers going around camp. Somehow we didn't mind the cold. I'd hear this old man going around the camp early in the morning. Still dark. "Bay-hah, bay-hah!" "Bay-zahn-day!" "Baht'-p'ehn-saw!" I asked Mom why this old man wakes everybody up, then he goes back to bed after waking everybody up. Told me he was the "camp crier." What's he crying about anyway! He done woke everybody up! She said he was telling everybody to get up, get movin, start cooking breakfast. Well, I'm gonna go to his tent and wake him back up. No, better not.

Us kids would see all the good gifts under that big Christmas tree and tell each other that so-and-so gift was probably "mine." Ooo! Bicycles, trucks, etc. Rats! When the Christmas service was finally over and Santa Claus and elfs started calling names out for gifts, we just knew we'd get that nice whatever, but, you know, I'd usually get a "corn bread" sock monkey. Or cherry chocolates and coloring book from the missionary barrel that was sent. But I got something, and Mom said I should be thankful I got that. Looking back, yeah.

I musta been about nine years old when, by golly, there was this long box Dad handed to me, all wrapped and pretty from the big Christmas tree. My dreams came true. I tore that thing open, and there "it" was. A brand-new Red Ryder thousand-shot lever-action BB gun. Like the old Winchester rifles you see in the old Western movies. Man, oh man! One thousand shots, not the old single shot I used to have. Even had Red Ryder gloves that had fringed cuffs. I didn't care for nothing else. Couldn't hardly wait 'til next morning. Mom was up before daylite, as usual, cooking breakfast. Soon as daylite came I was outta that tent, headed for bear or whatever. I went east toward and past the cemetery to a lil creek about three-quarters

10. Christmas encampment at Saddle Mountain Church, circa 1956. The 1951 Chevy (*front right*) belongs to the Tongkeamhas. Tongkeamha family photograph.

mile away. Seemed kinda far, but I gave it no thought. I was going to Africa. Well, I shot a redbird rite in the belly. Yeah that gun would do most fine. Funny how the years change you and other things. I wouldn't shoot a redbird now.

First thing Dad taught me about BB guns and any other gun was "safety." I can still hear him. No matter what, "It's always loaded." Do not ever point it toward something you are not going to shoot. It's not a toy. Make sure of the background toward where you're gonna shoot. A house, cow, a passing car, a person. Anything that may be behind the target you're shooting, etc. Never cross a fence with a gun, loaded or not. Do not shoot in or toward water. A lot of things to remember, but they come to me automatically. He would not tolerate carelessness. Keep it clean and out of sight. Good teacher.

I like to shoot rifles. Lil .22 to big caliber. I'm seventy-four now and still hunt on our old place. There's deer and elk now. When I was a lil guy I never dreamed there would be those kinda animals there. A few years ago the leaseman told me there were some buffalo on our place. Sure enough, I seen them. A cow and her three-year-old calf. I checked around, but nobody claimed them. They been there about six months, and I was told they weren't bothering other cattle, and it was okay to have them there. They would be mine, since nobody claimed them. I thought what if them two buffalo were Grandma and Dad somehow come back around? Woo. One day the leaseman told me that someone had shot them buffalo. Some white guy north of Carnegie. Sure got me mad. Heard a guy named GT told this white guy about them and took him out there. Don't know this T but heard he's bad for business. Lowlife.

All year long there seemed to always be a house full of different relatives would come and stay awhile. Don't know how but we always seemed to have something to eat. And room. We could always go rite down to the creek and catch a mess of fish or squirrels and rabbits. Summertime there would always be somebody out there. Swimming, fishing, playing ball, horse shoes, basketball, whatever. Mom had a big black caldron (vat) down there for laundry. Dad would build a fire under it to heat the water to a boil. Mom would have this yellow cake of lye soap (homemade). She would put in, plus our clothes. Her and others would turn those clothes around in there to clean. I remember that water was hot! Then they'd lift them out with the "turn" stick and put them in a tub. Drag it to the edge of the creek rinse and wring. I remember my sisters would take each end of an article of laundry, pull and twist in opposite directions to wring out water. Would even turn around doing it. Ha!

Grandpas, Grandmas, aunts, and uncles at different times would stay. I liked the cold winter mornings when I would wake to the smell of cedar smoking on the front-room woodstove. Grandpa or uncle rolling or smoking a cigarette. Before the sun came up, you could see the squirrels' silhouettes jumping through the leafless trees across the creek. It was so toasty warm and cozy. Plus, Mom would already have a hearty breakfast ready. And no, you couldn't just lay there and sleep a lil longer. Dad had you up and moving. So we've always been up before daylight.

We better have some kindling and wood chips in the box on the porch that morning, or else. Cutting wood, splitting it, carrying it to the house was a lot of work. We always had chores to do, before and after school. No inside plumbing, so we carried a lot of water from the creek. That would freeze up to about two or four inches thick sometimes, so we had to chop a hole through the ice for water. You had to hurry, or it would freeze up again. You had to go up the hill from the creek, and it was slick from snow and ice. Yes, you slipped down at times and had to go back for some more water. That creek provided many things for us. Water, fish, wood, pecans, swimming, games, shade, laundry, and a place to take off to when Mom got after you. "You gotta come home sometimes because you'll get hungry," was her parting words. Turns out we weren't too tough. If she couldn't reach us, Dad sure would.

Talking about fishing. We'd cut our fishing poles of "aet-tah-pohl" (locust) trees about an inch thick and about six or seven feet long. But no, Jughead had to cut his two or three inches thick. Man, you can't break that on no fish around there. He didn't care what size fish would bite. Even a slight nibble, and he'd say, "Got a bike," and rear back that club of a pole straight over his "Jug" head. That lil perch would be slammed to the ground behind him and not flop one bit. Dead on arrival man. But if he missed it, he shor would cuss. And you'd best not be behind him when he said "got a bike." You got a fractured skull if u did. So we stayed part ways from him. One time I told "Pug" Edmond Beartrack about how hard and sudden Jug jerked that pole! "Pug" cracked up the time I told him that jug jerked that pole so hard, but he thought he missed it (perch). He glanced at his hook and said he didn't lose his bait at least. I happened to glance at his hook and saw something on it alright but wasn't his bait. He jerked the lips right off that poor lil perch! Ha! I told "Pug" that there was a perch running around down there with no lips. "Pug" just cracked up.

One morning Pug Beartrack and Preston (Possum) Tonapahote came by and I guess asked Dad where the good fishing holes were. Dad told them, "Ask Raymond." I had my secret places to fish and wouldn't tell anyone. They were in the Army National Guard at the time when they asked me. I wouldn't give in at first. You know they bribed me. They had these sorta plastic helmet liners that go in steel helmets. Well, they told me I could wear one and put it on my head. I sure was liking it and sure 'nuff I told them my secrets. Same way in hunting. I wouldn't tell. I'm always asked "where." Dad would say, "Ask Raymond." Learned that from my big brothers, Stanley, David, and Chester Horse, plus Uncle Albert Cody and Burton Tonahcutt.

As a little guy, I always like to hang around those big guys and uncles. They were good outdoorsmen. Fishing, hunting, etc. They didn't quite like to take me along because I was small, but I was persistent. Anyway, after a while they'd decide to put up with me. I was kind of a daredevil and got into messes. I was trying to copy them but havin a hard time. Think they liked it. One day at Roy Horse's house, south of Uncle Cecil's, I heard them talking about going fishing. Boy, my ears perked up. I kept hintin around, but they acted like they didn't notice. Finally, I asked them could I go. They weren't too "on," but they told me I could go, but I had to catch some grasshoppers for bait. Man, there were all kinds of grasshoppers in that yard I noticed. Wouldn't take me long. I got a jar and filled it in no time. I was ready to go. You know, they just looked at me, and I'm like, "What'd I do?" Turns out they was the wrong kinda grasshoppers. What? They only used those yellow kind, about inch and a half long. All yellow or yellow with small black lines. Ha, at the time I didn't know but got some yellow ones this time and gone fishin. Some of the things I learned. One reason they probably didn't want me along was that I might make too much noise. So I learned to be quiet. And I'd get tired, hungry, and thirsty. I said I wouldn't, but I'd say anything just to go along. I'd tough it out long as I could, but they'd end up carrying me on their shoulders and lifting me over fences. They didn't seem to mind tho. Years later they would talk about it.

When it got lil too hot, I'd go to the creek, get in the water, and get ahold of a rock that could hold me under that cold water. I'd hold on to the rock while opening my eyes. Water was so clear. I'd watch the little crawdads, perches, and minnows. There used to be several kinds of little fish and bugs in that creek that you don't see anymore. Big three to four-inch rough-nose minnows that we called "stonerollers." One- to one-and-a-half-inch bottom-hugging type of minnow that we called just red, blue, and white minnows. They had a pointed nose and real tiny miniature shark tails. Their colors were of bright metallic. Pretty. They really didn't swim, just darted here and there. Hard to catch. Several kinds of sun perches. Mixed colors of red, orange, blue, white, black. Breams that we called "brims." They had beautiful metallic colors. Enjoyed watching them. Guess they disappeared too. When it rains enough to make the water rise again, all I see now are a few catfish, "goggle eye," which we called the perch with big eyes. Good eating. Their real name is "rock bass." Plus a few largemouth bass. Nothing like it used to be tho. Don't see any more jackrabbits, screech owls, mink, horny toads, bullfrogs, mountain boomers (collared lizards), prairie dogs. White man killing them off. Contaminate the land, water, and air. The country is my place of heaven on earth. I still go out there and camp by the creek for three or four weeks in summer. Summers are getting too hot now; water slows or quits running. Global warming is real.

I go out there in winter to hunt elk and deer. Mostly I'll just sit and take in God's beautiful creation. It's so peaceful and quiet. In that I seem to feel the presence of God. So still. "Be still and know that I am God." Psalm 46:10. My favorite reminder. I'm at peace. I think of all the people and things that went on out there. I'm not afraid or troubled. I'm home. It's all quiet now. But so many good memories. I thank God for providing me with that upbringing out there. I'm not alone or lonely out there. I'm with God. I've traveled a long way from there and seen and experienced many things, places, and people. I'd say to me, "Mom, I'm home now." "See, I'm playing in the water again." I thank my mom, dad, and grandma for who and what I am. My heroes. Taught me about God. My spiritual roots go back to that place I call "home." God willing, He'll take me to my real home, where my people dwell forever. I patiently and faithfully wait. Ah-ho [thank you].

Well, it's the year 2017 now. I'd have never believed I'd be around to see this. You know, I used to not pay any attention to the year numbers. Didn't know the numbers changed every year when I was young. Thought it would always be 1954 or something. Whoa. Every minute something changes. Yes, we get older. Supposedly, we learn more as we age.

Prayer meetings and prayer meetings were many for us. Just down the road in any direction would be a prayer meeting. A lot of relatives in the area then. Mostly all gone now. But that's what we knew. I remember a lot of the old ones. Good to hear all Kiowa hymns, prayers, testimonies. All spoke Kiowa. Good eats. Visits. Some prayer meetings were called "special" prayer meetings because it was for a special somebody or event. Birthdays or someone going away or coming home. Servicemen, etc. Anyway, these "specials" usually meant a big meal afterward. That's when more people showed up. A lot of them just sat in their cars until the service was over, then was first in line to eat. ☺ The other kind of meeting was called a "weekly" prayer meeting at different homes each week. Coffee, Kool-Aid, cookies, or cake were served afterward. Not too many showed up for those. Every time news of a prayer meeting was coming up, someone would ask, "Weekly or special?" The ones that showed up for "special" meetings were called "Sandwich Christians" according to Dad. ☺ Faithful few. There was a sorta elder, "K'on-ge-ohn' k'ēe," Black man, that came to those meetings with his guitar. Man, he could really get "into" it. Especially Holiness meetings. Called him "Brother Boone." We were at Grandma Isabelle (Horse) Kayitah's house about one and a half miles WNW of our house when I first saw him. I was about six or seven years old then. He got into his testimony with all the "twist N shouting" and guitar whanging, and, man, oh man, he was "into" it. I was sitting by Dad when he started in, and it seemed like this man was looking at me and singing and shouting at "me." Seemed to be dead serious. He even "jigged" around a little. Man, I got scared and eased behind Dad. ☺ But he seemed to get his message across. Later, as a teenager, I thought about him, and I thought, "You know, that Brother Boone Guy looked like 'Chuck Berry.'" Course he wasn't, but.

Getting back to Christmas at Saddle Mountain a bit. Guess I was into the Santa Claus thing. I was sitting between my big brothers, Wallace and Clifton, at Christmas nite service. It was packed. Wallace let me wear his red-and-black scarf, which I really did admire, I remember. Tucked in cozy between my big brothers. Safe and sound. Being Christmas nite, the service went on and on. I'd start to nod off, but one of my brothers would elbow me and quietly warn me not to, or I would miss Santa Claus. So I was really toughing it out. Sure didn't want to miss him.

Well, rats! I needed to use the bathroom (outhouse). It was outside the church, east. Just a tin walled-in, no-roof commode. Anyway, I kept telling my brothers, and they'd just look at me and scowl. "Hush, you don't need to." Finally convinced them I really did "need to go." They still looked at me with that "boy that guy" look. It was hard work squeezing thru all those people but finally made it out. Coming from that outhouse, I was nearing the church when I thought I heard someone say something. On that east side of the church was supposedly an empty space. No camps. I could hardly see and kinda scared. Then I did hear someone say, "P'AH-BEE." Yo! Everybody was in church. I heard it again and noticed a slight glow by the church. I could barely make out what seemed like a car. Sure 'nuff, I went to see, but nervous. Hey! It was Santa Claus sitting in a car! And smokin! He asked me what time it was and to tell them to hurry up. Buh! I don't know what time it was. You know what? Santa Claus had a mask on, and when he lifted it up and lit a match, man, oh man. Well, there it went. The Santa Claus thing.

It was Big P'ah-bee, "Bote T'ah-le" [Big Belly], Leon Redbone. ☺
After the "shock wave" I made it back thru the obstacle course and
by my brothers. I think they kinda figured something was buggin me
'cause Clifton would scowl at me and whisper, "What is it?" Finally,
as quietly as I could, I told him I seen Santa Claus. Boy, that look
he gave me! As quietly as he could he said, "Aw, you didn't either."
We were I guess quietly arguing. I said, "I did too see him. And he
was smokin!" Boy, oh boy, did I get a "quiet" elbow and that look.
Later they just cracked up. Anyhoo! But you know? There is a Santa
Claus. I call him God. He constantly brings me everlasting gifts of
life and joy! You better be good 'cause Santa Claus is watchin you!
"He's everywhere, He's everywhere!" Those were Christmases to
remember. No more like them.

Before I forget I need to mention the dog. Wallace's dog, our dog. I'm
not sure just when that dog showed up. Probably somebody dumped
it off up the road somewhere. I remember Mom and Dad trying to run
it off, but it wouldn't go too far. I guess if you seen the movie, "Ole
Yeller," well, that dog looked like that. After repeated attempts, that
dog wouldn't stay away. So Wallace claimed him as "his" dog after
Grandma sided with him. Course Mom laid down "her" law concerning
the dog's behavior. Leave her chickens alone, stay out of her flowerbeds
and the house. The dog said, "Okay." No, Wallace said that and named
him "Lucky." He took up for that dog, so it was his responsibility. But
Wallace always took up for animals. Had a soft spot for them that you
wouldn't know. And they became like "one." Inseparable.

That dog soon became well known to everybody that lived around
that area. He was gentle around everybody and oh so smart. He
looked up to Wallace with all his heart. Best hunting dog I ever
came to know or see. No squirrel or snake dog was better. And tuff?
That dog could fight. He would not fight unless told to by Wallace,
but Wallace didn't like for him to fight another dog. You couldn't
tell that dog had that in him. He was so protective of us kids and
family and so gentle. Coyotes, bobcats, 'coons, other strange dogs
soon found out to stay away from our area. Good watchdog. Didn't

bark much, but when he "treed" a squirrel down the creek, we had to go get the squirrel because Lucky wouldn't move until we did. And Lucky wouldn't "lie." If he "said" there was a squirrel in that tree, there was a squirrel in that tree. Sometimes you could not see one up there and swear there was no squirrel up there, but sure 'nuff there would be one. And he had to see if you did have it in hand. Sometimes we didn't want to go relieve Lucky but had to so he'd be satisfied. Even when it got dark. We had to convince him to leave his post, but he didn't like to.

Lucky always knew when a snake was around. Always patrolling. Kept us safe. He knew how to handle them. When confronting one, he'd find an opening to dart in and grab and just shake while biting it and just fling it away, dead. 'Course you couldn't tell which way he'd fling it, so you kept a safe distance, else you may have a snake necklace. One morning I was walking south thru the creek to a fishpond. At the edge of the creek and field was a cow trail along a fence. Our usual path. Lucky was always around somewhere. He'd pop up outta the brush now and then. Anyway, as I was ambling along the trail, I suddenly got hit behind the knees and flew to one side of the trail. I was shocked, scared, and mad. What the . . . ? I recovered and saw Lucky battling a big ole rattlesnake. Man, he saw it before I did and just knocked me out of the way. I didn't see him before that; just came out of nowhere, seemed like, but he'd been watching. There's so many things a body could say about that dog. Brave, tough, smart, humble, and a lot more.

The Bointys (Bill and Sally family) lived about two miles straight west of us. No telephones in those days. Oil lamps, woodstoves. No electricity. No TV, etc. But Mom and Sally Bointy could still communicate. They let each other know when a sewing, prayer meeting, or a visit was coming up. They had a "Lucky Express." Sure 'nuff, if Mom wanted to notify Sally about something coming up, she'd tie a note on Lucky's collar, talk to him, point toward the Bointys, tap him on the shoulder, and away he'd go. And Sally would answer Mom in the same way. For real!

Word got around about Lucky, and those white guys just had to see. They would bring their dog to challenge Lucky. We didn't like that; this wasn't a show. But they pushed Wallace to it. When somebody like that showed up with their dog, Wallace would get mad and tell them so. All the time Lucky would just lay on the porch. But kept his eyes on the dog. That dog would be prancing around in the yard, showing off and acting tuff. Lucky wouldn't move a muscle, just watched Wallace. When those guys pushed Wallace too far, he just said, "Sic 'em." And man, oh man. Lucky was on that dog in no time. Those dogs never had a chance. They'd be carrying or dragging what was left of their dog to their car or truck. One time Wallace was down the creek, north, fishing across the creek from where a guy named Elmer Jackson lived. He had a big white German shepherd dog. The creek was at full flood after a rain. Lucky was lying by Wallace across the creek from this guy, who was also fishing and had his dog.

After a while that guy accused Wallace of fishing on his land, which wasn't true. Then he started in bragging about his dog can whip Wallace's dog. That German shepherd kept growling and bouncing around on the other bank. Wallace didn't want to fight. The man accused Lucky of being afraid. So Wallace told him to bring his dog over, but the guy wouldn't because of the water. So Wallace said, "Get 'em!" Lucky jumps in that swift, flooding water; swims across; and whips the hell outta the guy's dog and swims back. Another time Grampa Tommy Catt pulls up in his truck with this great big German shepherd named "Hitler." Man! Well, he got Wallace mad, and he turned Lucky loose. So long "Hitler." Lucky was chewin on Hitler's leg, Wallace likes to say. Lucky seemed to be almost human. He understood things so well seems like. This story here is one of those times.

Wallace enlisted in the army for two years but ended up doing four years because the Korean War broke out. We had one of those big, tall, old radios that had tubes to run on. I remember when a tube burned out, we had to wait until we could get to town for one.

Glass bulb tubes. We got only about three or four stations, barely. Not too clear either, but it was a big thing. One day, when I was about seven or eight years old, James and I were walking thru the snow up to the main road to check mail. Anyway, I heard on the radio that our troops were having a hard time of it because the Chinese entered the war and were pushing back U.S. troops around that Chosin Reservoir.[7] Wallace's outfit (unit) was in the thick of it. I was pretty young, but I remember being scared for my brother. I told James but don't know if he understood what was going on. I told him I was going to Korea to help my brother. He just said, "Okay." Well, I could tell something was wrong around the house. A sorta tension. Us boys sleep in the north room, and I began to notice a weird, mournful sound outside our north window late at nite. Kinda scary. But I noticed Lucky wasn't quite himself lately. I was getting worried. Didn't quite grasp it.

Slowly I found out that Wallace was MIA (missing in action). And you know? Lucky knew. I think back to that time, and that's what Lucky was going thru. He was crying for his master. Sensed something wrong. I used to get mail from Wallace fairly often. He'd send me those pretty silk jackets with all the tiger and eagle designs on them from Korea and Japan and tell me to take care of my arm. He thought I might one day pitch baseball in the major leagues. Young as I was? He used to coach me at such a young age. But my mail dropped off. I was so down we'd have prayer meetings for him. Dad would sing War Mother songs at night, and I'd snuggle close to him. Where's my "Big" brother? Crazy, but I wanted to join up. Ha!

One day a big car drove up. Cadillac, I think. I see my uncle Edgar Doyebi get out and called to me. I went to him, and he had a big smile on his face. He patted me on the head and told me he had a surprise for me. Then I see this guy get out of that car with a big grin and in U.S. Army uniform. I was so overcome I don't kno what happened next. He lifted me up, and here comes Lucky. Boy, he was all over us just tumbling around. I don't know if I've ever been so happy. My hero was "home." Then Lucky gets Wallace by the wrist with his mouth and leads him across the yard to the house. Man, oh man! The next thing I did was grab my lil .22 single shot bolt-action rifle, and we were off to the creek and toward the "spring" to hunt some squirrels. He didn't even go into the house to change; we just took off. Wallace, Lucky, and I. What a beautiful and awesome God we have.

When hunting squirrels, sometimes things would get too hot for them when treed, and they'd take off jumping from tree to tree. We'd try to head them off, else they'd jump to the ground, where they'd get lost in thick brush or find a hole. But Lucky would be ahead of us, and, when that squirrel jumped for the ground, Lucky would be there and catch him in the air like a center fielder. I thought that was really something when I first seen that. When the creek water got low, there would be puddles here and there where water didn't run. Fish would be trapped there. We'd get a long limb and sweep thru the water with it to push them out. You could see their backs of mouths above water. Lucky would go one better. He'd jump in, grab them, and toss 'em on the bank. He'd even play ball with us, but we wouldn't let him bat. ☺ He'd catch fly balls or run the grounders down with his glove (mouth).

One time Wallace was walking by the old high school building in Carnegie. A man was trying to get a dog to get in the trunk of his car. He had a rope on the dog, and the dog didn't want to get in that trunk. The man had a club and was cussin and hitting that dog. Well, Wallace goes over and tells him to quit hitting that dog like that. That guy turns and cusses Wallace out. Oh boy, Wallace just beats that guy up pretty bad and takes the dog. He just don't like to see a dog mistreated like that.

Grandpa Winston Catt would get up early in the mornings and go down to the creek for a while. I wondered why he did that. So I asked Mom. She said, "Ask him." So I did. Ha, he said when he goes down there those "Lil People" tell me, good morning! I said, "Zame-t'ay"; there ain't no Lil People down there. "I don't believe you, Grandpa," I said, and I'm going with you next time. He just smiled a little and said, "Okay." Boy I was up 'specially early the next morning. We went down there, and he rolled a cigarette, smoked some and "daw-t'syed" (prayed). We walked toward the water and stopped. Then we went closer to the water. Then he said, "Ah-b'ohn," as we edged closer to the water's edge on the little muddy bank. Sure 'nuff, there was these lil peoples raising their hands up as we advanced. "K'ee'dah t'sy-g'yah." Good morning. Crawdads! ☺ They'll do that when you get close to them while backin up. Raise their pincers up. He had me there. He'd always go down there, winter or summer, smoke, pray, greet the Little People, and wash his face. There's a lot of things we don't notice. Especially nowadays. Take your time. If you hurry like "hell," you'll probably get there. Bay-t'oh-bay, nay, baht-t'aw-yaw, naw daw-k'ee ah-daw. "Be still, and know that I am God." Psalm 46:10. Haw! T'sol-haw! G'yah-oh-boy-dah. It's true.

I have this thing about mountains. Rocky, little, sparse-treed hills and big mountains. I seem drawn to them somehow. I just want to be there. When I was younger, I'd go south of our place, past Old Jim Tracey Ranch, where the mountains start. Beautiful place in there. Canyons branch off into others. Up toward the top of one of them was a sorta long bench-like rock ledge. When I reach that, while hunting, I'd sit down to rest a bit. Wind blowing in my hair, alone with my thoughts, I talk to God. Peace is here. Nobody but God knows I'm here. I have a lot of thoughts. I can see part of Carnegie, Mountain View, and Fort Cobb. I know I must go down into that some-kinda world someday. Kinda don't want to tho. Not just yet. Then I'd get up and start back. Come on, dog; let's go down into that cruel world.

Several times when I travel up north, New Mexico, Colorado, Wyoming, Utah, Idaho, Montana, even Canada, I feel more and more at home in those mountains. I feel the pull. Bold, clear streams; lodge-pole pine; quaking aspen trees; etc. I can't get enough of them and hate to head back. When I'm among them with my Indian tapes on, I like to imagine them still singing the old songs and dancing somewhere deep in those mountains like they did before the cancer (whiteman) showed up. I feel I belong there. I love their powwows. They are so traditional. Keep their old ways intact. Real ones. Sometimes I think maybe I shoulda stayed up there with my Crow family. They've asked me, of course. But I wouldn't want to leave my family and my people jus for my own selfishness. Been up there many times but wonder if I'll ever go again. Just one more time? We Kiowa came from northern Montana next to Canada. About thirty-five miles south of Canada is a place called Kiowa, Montana. Visited there a few times. Awesome. Just think, my people were there. We were mountain Kiowa one time. The old "Kiowa Mountains" are in northern Wyoming. We were of the "T'ho-k'ope," Cold Mountains. Rockies maybe. That's why I feel that "pull" when I'm there.[8]

Walking was the way of travel for many of us back then. Some had cars. We mostly had a car. Maybe it was broke down, and Dad would walk to work and back, two miles west to Ed Dietrich's, mile and half to Jim Tracey's. Sometimes he's come home for lunch on a horse, jeep, or tractor. Course we'd ride with him to the road on his way back. Was something to us. But Dad was a pretty good mechanic and usually kept the car going. Was always tinkering with his car. He said, "In those days, all you needed to keep a car going was a pliers and some bailing wire." Not so nowadays. Sell you a car made out of plastic and charge the hell outta you. Giemausaddle boys, Dave and Bobby, would walk six miles to our place to play. Hokeahs, four miles; Bointys, two miles; Bread and Tsatoke boys, one and a half miles; Lincoln and Gerald Meat, two and a half miles. Eagle Heart Spring was two and a half miles north of our place. Fritz Kaulay, one and a half mile north of us. We'd all meet at Fritz's creek on our way to Eagle Heart with our cold biscuits and commodity spam meat. Swim all day, walk back home. There was always something to do along the way. If you got tired or hungry, "you were jus blowed up." Dave Giemausaddle said they'd try to get back home before the "saw-poles," owls, came out. ☺ I used to take some dried meat with me when I'd be gone hunting. Keeps you going, our "go power."

One time on our way to Eagle Heart Spring, we were walking

thru the water in the creek that goes that way to keep cool; Spi and I, well, we spied a lil squirrel in a low tree, and, being the great hunters we were, we gave chase. I flung a stick at it as it jumped thru the branches and nailed it dead. It was such a lil guy squirrel that we felt we shouldn't have killed him. After all, we weren't really hunting, and it was summer. Wrong time. Anyway, we were feeling bad about it. We sat down and said, "What shall we do with it?" So I suggested a funeral for the lil squirrel. We dug a grave and put him in it. Put some wild flowers on it. Spi suggested we get a marker or cross. I said, "What shall we put on it?" I found a flat rock and etched on it, "Here lies Fuzzy." Anyway, he got a proper burial and a name. Well, Big P'ah-bee Wallace is usually spying on us. Anyway, one morning Spi and I were sitting on the porch talking about what was on our agenda that day. What shall we do, etc. We didn't know it but he (Wallace) was standing inside the screen door listening. All of a sudden we heard him say, "What about 'Here lies Fuzzy?'" Well, our funeral wasn't too secret. Guess he followed us and seen our grave. Man, that guy! But he liked to "track" us at times just to nose.

We weren't too tuff, I guess, 'cause we got our poison ivy, bee and ant bites. Mom had this stuff she used for bleach in her laundry, I guess. She called it "bluing." Anyway, every time we got bit, we got doused with this bluing. We'd be running around with these blue splotches on us. One time Spi and I had such a bad case of poison ivy that was made worse by scratching. Swollen eyes and we were covered by this lotion Mom put on us. Man, that stuff turns white. We were running around with white all over us. Australian Aborigines? Kinda like that. In winter Vicks was the cure-all. But we didn't like it. Or castor oil. We'd be running around coughing, hackin up "green ones," and snotty noses. All at once Grandma would grab one of us, flop you, and before you knew it you had your throat punched with a big gob a Vicks. We'd run off gagging in protest. An unexpected "pit stop" and a "Vicks fix." For whatever ails you. Then we'd run to and get on the Alden school bus smelling like bote [tripe]. Good ole days!

About nine miles south and one mile east from Carnegie was the town of Alden. A two-story building, a blacksmith shop, garage-gas station, and German church. And about three or four houses was Alden town. That two-story building housed a doctor and dentist on top and a general store on the bottom. That general store had everything u needed for then. Groceries, candy, shoes (brogans) or "bull hides," clothes, tools, ammo, cotton sacks (ugh), and just about anything u needed. Incidentally, that doctor there "borned" Dad there. Dad was born there, and the doctor's name was Dr. Weiser. ☺ So all those Germanys (white guys) and some of my uncles around there called Dad "Doc." I used to wonder about that name. Known to those around there as the hardest-working, honest, ball-player (baseball), dedicated person around. About six foot three, two hundred pounds, with no fat. Seems like he can do about anything. Also local auto mechanic and barber. Kiowa hymn singer and deacon at Saddle Mountain.

Anyway, right straight east, one mile was our school of Alden Eagles. First thru twelfth grade at one time. I went there to ninth grade. In 1958 I went to Carnegie, as Alden dropped tenth thru twelfth grades because of low attendance. Kept the grade school for a while, I guess. For our grade level we had a pretty good basketball team. I think, won about all our games for about three years. Me, Francis (Jake) Chalepah, Wallace Bitseedy, Thurman Kaulaity, Gerald Meat, and Albert Oyebi. Today you would never know a town or school was there. No evidence. Pasture now. But it was a good-sized school with big gym and auditorium.

Gerald and Lincoln Meat and I would ride to Alden on horseback if we had a dime and some pennies for firecrackers or a candy bar that had a big shiny ring on top. Cost five cents just to get that ring that this shine peeled off about fifteen minutes later. Act "hoss" for lil while anyway. People would ask me later about what we did on Saturdays out there. I said "drag main" on horseback. Lotta good memories about Alden. Hah, we used to terrorize those German hillbillies. 'Specially Gerald and Lincoln, as they were big guys.

Gerald had to order a special-size basketball trunks because of his big "zile" [rear end]. But he was a good ballplayer. He used to catch for me when I pitched. Others were scared to. I threw pretty hard then.

I would walk to the house at times when I seen a strange car sitting outside. There would be some white people there talking to Dad and Mom. Later they would tell me those were people from other schools around there. Coaches, principals, trying to figure a way for me to attend their school to play ball for them. But it couldn't be done. I didn't want to anyway. I'd heard some and noticed some things about Carnegie people before but really seen it when I started school there. For one thing the white guys that were kinda good friends to us at Alden turned away from you at Carnegie. They were now among their kind. But that wasn't the big thing. Prejudice showed its ugly head. That coach, for whatever reason, didn't like me. He wanted me there, but I seen his jealousy. The second year I was there he called the basketball players out on the court. I didn't smoke, but he threw a pack of cigarettes on the floor and said they were in my locker. I'm off the team. Before that Dad bought me some new Converse All-Star basketball shoes, which somebody promptly stole. I'm sure if he didn't do it himself, then he had somebody do it. Those white people didn't want an Indian boy taking their baby boys' place on the team. I was a starter on baseball, football, and basketball, and they made it hard for me. After team practice, whatever it was, I'd walk or hitchhike home. Some of those white guys I went to school with at Alden or were on the team lived south of town but zoomed on past me in their cars. But I expected it. But it didn't sit right with Mom or Dad. That was my first year there (sophomore).

One day in study hall, before football practice, Mom left a note at school for me. Said I now had a car and where it was parked. I was pretty happy about that. Now I had a ride. And so did my p'ah-bees after practice and games. A nifty 1953 Chevy two-door hardtop with whitewall tires, spoked wheel covers, radio with front and back speakers, back fender skirts. White on top and yellow on bottom. Those Horse boys called it the "Lightning Bug."

White people in Carnegie and everywhere else will never change. I don't like them of course because of the way they think, so that's the way they do. I just tolerate them; so did Dad. One day Dad said, "Whiteman is gonna outsmart himself." That is so true. Identity theft, fraud, spying on you, and much, much more. They make these things, and these things turn right around and bites him in the ass. Then he (whiteman) invents another gadget that he says will protect you from that. Same thing happens. There is no cure for that. They're just feeding the hackers; it's a game to them. He created a monster. Ads on TV. Bombard you with all these medicines and gadgets that are a sure cure for whatever ails you, then turns right around and tells you the hundreds of ways these can kill or cancer you. Then he snows you with all the insurance companies that you can buy to sue these people. "You may be entitled to ___, call this number now." Well, this whiteman is pretty sick himself from greed, and there is no medical cure for that. He reminds me of that story of this King Midas and his greed for gold so that everything he touched turned to gold. Well, everything the whiteman touches turns to saw-g'yah (s —— t)! And that is so true. G'yah-oh-boy-dah! These kinda statements could literally go on forever.

I remember Dad telling us about this big cattleman, rancher whiteman he worked for about a mile and half south of us. Jim Tracey had a lotta land and cattle. Jim Tracey Ranch. Anyway, it was around 1964 [1965], I think. Dad was working for him. Cowboying. That evening (news time on TV) Dad came to the barn, through for the day. As he was getting off his horse, he heard a door slam and noticed Jim Tracey headed toward him hollerin. He was moving pretty fast for somebody his size and age. Dad was tired and was taking his time seeing to his horse. This whiteman was running around following Dad and hollerin about what was on the news he was watching. Dad just took his time. Blacks were rioting and burning in California (Watts, LA). Mr. Tracey just kept on jumping and hollering. Doc, Doc, these n —— s are rioting and burning our cities down. What we gonna do Doc? Doc, what we gonna do? Finally,

Dad got through with the horse business and turned to Jim Tracey and said, "Jim, *you* brought 'um here!" Well, that whiteman just shut up and turned back to his house. Dad said, "Yeah, I heard him the first time." When Dad asked a whiteman about somethin, and they didn't quite know or what to say about it, they'd just hesitate with "well . . . well." Dad would say, "Well? A well is a hole in the ground!" Zame-t'ay! Or when some old whiteman he knew died, someone would ask what happened. Dad would say, "Don't know, he just laid down and died, I guess."

Out in the country at our house and about half mile north of our mailbox is an intersection. West to Green Valley and Saddle Mountain and north to Carnegie. Can't tell now, but there was a gas station and lil grocery store called "Peaville Corner." A baseball diamond was also there.[9] Right west of there lived George and Floyd Steckman. Two houses. George Steckman owned that station. Pretty big guy, approx. six foot three and 250 lbs. One bigoted, prejudiced piece of s——. One day Dad took his mom, Fannie (my grandma), to that store to cash her t'sown-awlan-khoot (grass money check).[10] Guess Mr. Steckman didn't know Dad was around when Grandma indicated to him she wanted to cash her check for some groceries. This Steckman called her a gut-eater, and he didn't cash gut-eater checks. About that time Dad walked in and heard it all. Dad said, "You Red Ass, you called my mother a gut-eater?" And proceeded to beat the whiteman to a pulp. Jughead sho liked that. We all did. This lowlife eventually moved to Carnegie. He had two sons that were just like him. The devil's spawn. This country here in 2017 has a president of the same spawn. And I wonder what's wrong with this country. Ignorant, blind greed.

Back to younger days and ways. The old tall, wood-panel, small dial radio was our connection to the outside world. In it was our movies or TV and music. One or two stations during the day. Maybe three or four at nite. We listened to episodes in a series like *Amos 'n' Andy* Black comedy. Sgt. Preston of the Royal Canadian Mounted Police and his dog, King. Or the Shadow knows. Green Phantom.

Wooo! Plenty scary then. This was all on radio, but we could see it clearly in our minds and actually seemed real. We didn't know what a movie theater was. Or a movie-star show.

The music was mostly country and western. Saturday nite we gathered round the radio to listen to the *Grand Ole Opry*. Barely hear it at times. I'd be walking across the fields on my way home from or going fishing with these songs in my head and still remember Jimmy [Jimmie] Rodgers and his songs of the Railroad Hard Times was Dad's favorite. Yodeling Jimmy Rodgers. Hank Thompson, Hank Snow, Hank Williams, Faron Young, Webb Pierce, Lefty Frazelle [Frizzell], Bob Wills and Texas Playboys. Roy Acuff. I like to listen to Merle Haggard or George Jones. Boogie-woogie, blues, rhythm 'n' blues, rock 'n' roll oldies are my favorites. Also will listen to Cajun and zydeco from Louisiana, having been there.

If people my age and older were to tell young ones today how things were in our day, they probably wouldn't believe it. They couldn't comprehend anything other than what's here today. Like back in the day when all cars were black at one time. Wind up record players. Phonographs and records—45, 78, 33⅓, 16½ sizes, rpm. Eight-track players to no telling what now. All roads were dirt and gravel.

A lot of neighbors and relatives were just down the road. Most of those houses are gone with the wind and the way things were. You didn't need to lock your doors at nite, or if you're gone all day or two. If somebody came to your house needing something, and you weren't home, it was understood that you took what you needed. Salt, sugar, coffee, flour, even water or bread. Sometimes people would leave something in place of what they took. Money, wood put up, water buckets full, or foodstuff. They looked out for each other and took only what was reasonable. Course they told you about it later on when you got back from wherever we went; when we got back, the first thing Dad noticed was tire tracks. "Somebody's been here," he'd say. Think he knew everybody's tire tracks.

And this. Every Sunday morning about nine thirty we'd hear this droning sound for a couple minutes. Then a hard "whap!" It was our Sunday paper being delivered by airplane, hence the plane's drone and newspaper hitting the ground in the yard.[11] When Dad heard that sound, he'd holler at us kids to "get in the house!" 'Course we wanted to watch the plane, but no way. We never actually thought about the weight of that newspaper and the impact of hitting the ground. Hardheaded as we were, we woulda been dented for life. Grandma couldn't read, but she liked to look at the comics. Guess she could read those. Especially Dick Tracy. ☺ Dad worked for rancher Jim Tracey down the road, but, when that paper came, first thing Grandma would ask for was Hy-yah-b'ah, Jim Tracey? Where is Jim Tracey? She wanted that Dick Tracy part of the paper.

Straight east of our place about a mile, two creeks over, lived an old white woman by herself. A big, old yellow frame house by a creek. Grandma's friend. Dad would drop Grandma and me off there while he plowed nearby. All I knew her by was Miss Aunt Deel or Deal. They would sew and visit somehow, as Grandma didn't speak much English. I wondered at that. Anyway, I was about five or six years old and liked to fish. A big red barn nearby had a buncha worms under the damp straw. Right below the house was a big cottonwood tree, which sat on the very edge of the bank. Kinda hung over the bank. Kinda deep there and, man, it was good fishing. I'd stand on the edge of the bank and drop my bait straight down. No waiting. You had a bite. Sometimes Grandma would sit with me to help. She'd warn me not to venture away from her sight. Well sir, I still fish there today and still catch fish there. It seemed to always had fish.

One evening I was fishing there when Mr. Don Orrell drives up. The owner who lets me fish on his place. I told him about me and Grandma fishing same place when I was about five or six. I'm still doing it. He was amazed about that and how much I knew about that area and the people then. All the guys that used to be with me there are gone. Many stories there. Here's one: me, Wallace, James, Bro Spi, Snake [Kenneth Methvin], and Bruce were hunting there. We spied a big 'coon way up this pecan tree. We surrounded the tree and shot our "n —— shooters" (slingshots) or threw rocks at it. I noticed Spi (Herman) bending over at the base of that tree, looking for ammo, I guess, when somebody scored a direct hit on the 'coon, and it dropped outta that tree and hit the ground right next to Spi's leg. That thing was madder than hell and came up swinging. Oh man, Spi was making some kinda unearthly, ungodly, unhuman sounds while dancing and shaking a tail feather. We think he coulda won any world championship Fancy War Dance contest. Tuke Koomsa, Tugger Palmer, Johnny Whitecloud, or Elmer "Sugar" Brown would not have had a chance against "Spi" Methvin that day. We all 'bout died laughing. It was so funny! Course Spi wasn't too "on" about that. We did not know he or somebody could move that fast or make those kinda sounds. Snake said he was gonna enter Spi at the Indian fair contest. That cat can move, I guess.

I heard from people that Grampa [Kiowa Jim] walked to Saddle Mountain Church from our house. That's quite a walk. Probably around seven or eight miles over some pretty rough country. Up and down over big hills we called mountains. How many times he did, I don't know. He had a wagon and team and maybe a Model T car and horses, but maybe something happened to them. A dedicated deacon he was. I did the same thing one time, but no more.[12] Wild country back there. 'Bout a six- or seven-hour walk. I know his first church Kiowa hymn. Only one knows it, I guess. Saddle Mountain was straight southwest of our house.

Dad told me a pretty powerful story about his dad, Grandpa. How real and powerful God is. Apparently, Grandpa was a pretty strong believer and leader in the Peyote Road. And so was Frank, Dad's brother who was older than Dad. They were pretty well known in Peyote circles around the area and other tribes, especially the Otoe tribe around Red Rock, Oklahoma. They were often asked to run meetings and doctor. Otoes thought a lot of them. I remember Dad and Mom would make the trip to Otoe Powwow. I had no idea where Red Rock was, but just the two would go. When they got back, they would be loaded down with stuff. Blankets, shawls, and other items. The Otoes still remembered Grandpa and gave away to Mom and Dad these things.

Well, one day Uncle Frank got sick and slowly got worse. I imagine they took him to a doctor or doctored him Indian way, but to no avail. They then took him to a whiteman's hospital, where the doctor said nothing could be done. So Grandpa took Uncle Frank home to die, I guess. Now Grandpa thought the world for Frank and would do anything for him. He didn't want to lose him. Frank knew he was going to die, and he told Grandpa, "Dad, I'm going on now. Doctors told me that." Well, Grandpa burst into tears and would not believe it. He kept telling Frank that "no, you're not going to die, you'll be alright." But Frank knew and kept telling Grandpa that. Grandpa said, "No, I'll never see you again if you die." But Frank told him, "Yes, you'll see me again." Grandpa did not believe him and said, "How can I see you again if you die?" Well, Frank told Grandpa, "You quit what you're doing, and you'll see me again." He meant the Peyote Road. Here, I'm sure, sometime during Frank's illness, a minister of the Jesus Road had talked to him about life after death. If you repent, quit doing what's not on the Jesus Road. Or other things God considers sinful. *"Thou shall not have no other gods before me." "You shall not take for yourself an idol in the form of anything in Heaven, above or on the earth." "You shall not bow down to them or worship them; for I, the Lord your God, am a jealous God,"* punishing the children for the sin of the fathers. Frank had taken Jesus Christ as his lord and savior and wanted his dad to do the same. And Grandpa did. The Jesus Road over the Peyote Road. He, Grandpa, destroyed everything connected to Peyote and took up the cross to Saddle Mountain Indian Baptist Church, where he became a deacon and buried there with rest of the family.

Dad, of course, knew about Peyote but never was involved or practiced it. I'm the same way. The Jesus Road is the *only* road there is. I will have no other road. I've always seen Peyote Road as a means to skirt the real issue. They call it a church to skirt legal issues. The things that go with it are earthly things. Not of the spirit. They think they're more Native American than you are. Or more traditional. They say, "God put these things on earth for us to use." Yes, He did. But He meant for them to be used the right way, but that decision was up to you. Go back to the Garden of Eden. God gave us a mind (brain) to reason (think, choose) with; He didn't make the choices. We do that. This prayer says it better. *"God, grant me the serenity to accept the things I cannot change. Courage to change the things I can. And the wisdom to know the difference."* Covers everything. We Native Americans have our traditions, culture, that go way back. They identify us. But some of them we can't use in "God's world." And we know that. Any substance that alters the mind that's of the earth not the spirit is against God's laws. You can be traditional and keep it through God's word. Earthly things don't mean anything in the final analysis. If I need something (substance) that will get me high enough to God's level or think and feel I am, then I am going to have a long, hard fall. I don't need that. I or anybody else can have church (worship) anywhere we choose. Big church, lil church, bedroom, car, wherever, I stop and talk to Him. I don't need anything on earth to feel or see God's presence.

Remember, peyote is something of the earth, not of the spirit. A drug that will get you high. A false awareness of God's presence. A quarter-moon-shaped altar made of earth. Peyote is placed there with a drum, beaded staff, gourd rattle, tobacco, other material things. Then they attend a Baptist, Methodist, or Pentecostal church they say they're members of. You cannot serve God and Man, earthly things. It cannot be done according to God's law. They even bring their Peyote blankets, gourd, and songs to "God's house" at one's wake and funeral services. WWJD? What would Jesus do? I, and others I'm sure, are not comfortable with that.[13] The Anti-Christ is hard at work. Dad used to say, "The devil sits in every church." I didn't get it at first.

I seen how this works. In the early eighties or late seventies, Dad had his (our) house out in the country remodeled. It looked really nice. Even had in-door plumbing for the first time and adding a big bathroom with a shower and big bathtub. Wow! Dad bought a one-and-a-half-acre lot and build a house two and a half miles SE of Carnegie. To please Mom. It about killed him to move to town. He didn't like town life, and I know he wasn't happy. Think he was gonna move out there.

I lived in Dallas at the time. Anyway, there's this grandson of Mom who had been asking Mom could he and his family rent the newly remodeled house. Adelaide Tonemah Little Chief's grandson, David Quertebitty. Known to us as "Boley." Had a Cheyenne wife. Don't think he was kin to Dad, but Dad knew all about him, as we all did. The kinda guy that won't work but can BS. Didn't amount to anything to me. This guy actually begged and cried to Mom to get Dad to rent that house to him since she was his grandma. Dad did not want him there because this goofball was a Peyote man, and Dad told him so. This damn guy kept it up until Dad gave in to Mom. Dad finally said, okay, only under certain conditions. Dad warned him about the use of peyote in any form or practice. And he better not see a teepee or a Peyote meeting there or he's out! 'Course Boley said he wouldn't do those things there.

I don't know how long Boley was there. Dad told the neighbor up at the highway to call him if he ever sees a teepee there. Well, after a while he did. Dad beats it out there, and sure 'nuff there was a teepee set up down there. Dad didn't waste no time. He was pretty pissed. He reminded Boley that it wasn't very long ago that he told him not to do that and to start packing, as he had thirty days to get off his place or he would burn his teepee down. Of course, Mom caught it too. Not long after that Dad's house burned down. Everything. The neighbor told Dad that he seen two cars leaving with stuff, and two days later the house was in flames. Uncle Pat Oyebi lived in Dallas at the time and hated to tell me why, but I needed to go or call home. I was about to find out why. But I was soon shocked completely through. I would not believe it. Just numb. Not my house! My temple!? Well, I couldn't bring myself to go home. To what? It's gone!

Maybe it was a good thing this guy died before I got ahold of him. Mom knew that. God is a jealous God and doesn't want us to worship any other kind of god but Him. I seen that. This guy brought the devil to our house. He paid for it alright, but at what a price. Peyote, in any form, has no business in God's house. Whether it be Baptist or Methodist. We need to speak up. These days are gone, but God's word will be here forever. I have brothers and friends that partake of that, but I just do not believe that way. They try to justify Peyote, but hopefully one day they'll see it before it's too late. Pride stands guard.

## June 2019 Narrative

I don't know how or where Mom and Dad got married. I heard it was arranged by my uncle Cecil Horse, who was married to Dad's sister, Jennie Haumpy Horse. Or one of my grandpas, Tommy or Winston Catt. Knowing that Dad was a hard worker and who had parents who were well known and affluent. I don't think Mom knew they had plans for her or who Dad was. It was the "old way" I guess. The story was that she was taken to Grandpa's ranch and just dropped off. Lol! Everybody knew but her, I guess. Of course, she was pretty scared. That's something I heard, but I think Mom confirmed it. God blessed them with many things.

Mom was a wise, strong, talented, spiritual, compassionate, hard disciplinary, and a hard-working woman. Not just because she's my mother I'm saying this. I'm who I am through her. I'm so grateful for such a mother. I know we gave her a hard time sometimes, but she proved herself to us. We knew our place. She was so schooled and knowledgeable about the old Kiowa ways and language. I wish I could remember at least some of the oh so wonderful or humorous stories she told us. Trails have grown dim.

Out in the pecan grove, plum grove, cotton fields, or yard landscaping, she'd be right there with us. But I threw my towel in when she came out of the kitchen and got in on our basketball game. Lol! She still had flour on her hands. ☺! I didn't know she played basketball at Rainy Mountain, Fort Sill, and Riverside Indian Schools. Even heard she was a dead shot with a basketball. She also played softball with us. Momma mia!

I don't think I've seen better beadwork than hers. And I've been to a lot of different tribal powwows. I have seen it copied in design and colors though. I can always tell if that's the case. It's all over the world. I'd think her designs are all in her head. No drawn-out patterns, etc. Sad, I know her designs are lost now. Covered over.

She also sewed a lot. I remember her old foot-pedal Singer sewing machine. Made and repaired our clothes. She also crocheted. I remember the full dresses she made for Lavena and Melissa. One was white, the other red. We thought they were classics. She altered, patched our clothes for what she liked to call "everyday clothes." So what were our "go to town clothes?" Well, we hardly ever go to town. We just sent in our wishes for whatever. We had to go in shifts whenever we did. Fighting over whose turn it was to go. I didn't care that much for town. We shopped at our neighbor's dump. Our first Wal-Mart.

Mom loved little fishes and always had a little fishbowl with three or four goldfish, about two inches long. Here's a true story about her love for them. As stated, we always camped for Christmas at Saddle Mountain and into the next New Year. And it was pretty cold back in those days. Dad would make a trip back to the house now and then for whatever. Anyway, one time we were moving back to the house, and it was cold. Dad started to get the front-room woodstove going, and I noticed Mom hurrying to get the kitchen woodstove fire up first thing. We were busy moving things back into the house and to keep warm. After some time I heard Mom hollering around in Kiowa and sounded like praying. We didn't know she got the kitchen woodstove fired up. It had an oven, and when she opened it, she took out a bundled white towel. In the towel were three goldfish flopping around. The fourth one was dead. I guess she checked on her fish first thing and seen they all froze in the bowl. Out of desperation and, I'm sure prayer, she wrapped and placed them in the oven. Dad couldn't believe it, nor I. We all just stood still and stared. Not Mom, she went right on with her usual ways like she knew all along what she was doing and singing. A miracle? When Dad gets surprised, and he doesn't too often, he'll say, "Sa-a-ay or say!" "Them things is alive." I've told people about that at times, and of course some don't believe it. How long were they froze?

Mom was of the old order of things. She was raised by these older Kiowas and knew their ways. People ask me today where did she get those stories and songs. Well, she lived it through a Kiowa war chief's son and daughter-in-law. They are being taught today. She also loved birds and had two parakeets. She liked to watch the wild birds out of her kitchen window and fed them. One snowy winter day I looked and seen all these birds on the ground by the house, feeding. You might know me, hah. Well, I saw "a redhammer" male flicker, and I figured I needed those feathers; so I snuck out to the carport with my .22 mag and nailed the bird. Also just then the kitchen door burst open, and the heavens open up with all the fury with Mom leading the onslaught. I also got nailed. I did not know she was watching while doing dishes. Talk about somebody testifying; you shudda heard me. Those were her birds and you'd best know that.

Also, one especially snowy winter, when most birds have a hard time of, they come close to the house for maybe a handout. I was about eight years old I guess. About fifteen feet in front of the porch was a whole flock of birds feeding in the snow. I suddenly had a great idea. I'm gonna catch me one of those pretty redbirds. What to do with it if I did get one, I didn't know. Just see if I could. I got a long string from Mom's sewing stuff, which I knew was off-limits to my, no-telling-what projects. Anyway, I made a slip noose on the end to snare the bird. I strung it out to where they were feeding and thru a small crack in the door. I knelt down and watched thru that small crack. Then, out of nowhere, came this thunder and lightning. Mom, with her wet dish towel, popped my "zile" with it. My "bisquits" were probably showing 'cause, boy, that hurted. Even quail come close at those times, but I'd better not shoot one. She liked to eat them but not see how we got them.

I thank her for seeing us thru the oh so cold and snowy winters. It doesn't snow like it used to, nor get as cold today. Sometimes our road up to the highway would be snowdrifted over. Couldn't get out until the snow melted and the melt dried. Mom always had hot meals for us and somehow kept us clean, though she had no washer or dryer. She had her big tubs and kettles and rub-board. Also she would pull out her canned stuff from the garden or from the canned wild plums and 'possum grapes she put up last summer. Along with her big hot biscuits, we were just fine. For treats she made hard candy and donuts. Sometimes she put pecans or walnuts in the candy, which was a real treat.

I sorta seen her one time doing something but didn't bother to ask. We were waiting out a storm in the cellar one time, I noticed she had this, what looked like a gallon jar, wrapped in a towel and shaking it. A little later she handed it to one of my sisters, who did the same thing. Then it came my turn. So I shook the thing 'til my arms tired, then handed it off. The next one did the same thing. Finally, I asked her what that was all about. Was it some kinda game. Dumb me. She said, "No, it's our butter or cheese." Or cottage cheese. Sure enough, milk from the milk cow turns into butter when you shake it long enough. I'm so glad I was raised by a mom that is a strong Christian. I probably wouldn't be here right now but for her showing me the way thru our father in heaven. Made sure we were clean and presentable for church. Sunday inspection. She reminded us that our manners and appearances reflected to others what kind of mother and father we have. "If you can't say anything good about others or something, don't say anything" was her byword. It follows me today. Even though, being human, it gets tough to do, but I'll remind myself of that.

There are actually people out there that don't [feel] that they need anybody. Go it alone. Or don't feel the need to read "the instructions." If you don't have God in your life, you have nothing. We were always up early so we had time for God. Before we broke bread, Dad would read from the spiritual pamphlet, *The Upper Room*. Every morning at breakfast Mom had a scripture from the Bible written on a piece of paper, which she handed to each one of us kids to read. And you had to. I'd almost forgot about this until here lately when my niece Shirley Nickell mentioned it. Shirley is the daughter of sister Peggy Tongkeamha Nickell. We had a different scripture to read each day. For something we'd have to say what we wanted at the table in the Kiowa language. She'd say, "How can you say you're Kiowa if you don't speak it." Grandpa Winston was the same way. He'd really get on to us if we spoke to him in whiteman way. Especially when we'd ask him for aw-law-gyah, money. He'd say, "P'ae-gaw (again), there you go, talking that stinkin whiteman trash." "You keep talking like that, your mouth will rot off!" Yo! And Grandma used to warn me about drinking coffee when I was a little guy. In Kiowa she'd say, "Don't you drink coffee; you'll turn black and grow whiskers." Yo! Scared me.

Mom and her sisters would come down to the creek to cool off in the water when the day heated up. A bunch of us kids would already be in the water a ways from them. I used to wonder about the kind of noise coming from their way. A kinda deep, Pah-doomp, Pah-doomp! Deep popping sound, they'd be sitting down waist deep in the water with dresses on. Anyway, they'd flatten their palms, fingers tight together; stretch out their arms; and hit the water like slicing it. Their hands would go straight down hard and about a foot and a half, then cross over each other. Do this hard enough, and it makes that sound. Ha! Boy, we thought that was funny. We'd try it but weren't good at it. So I asked Mom why they did that. She said, "It's to scare the snakes, turtles, and water moccasins away."

I barely remembered a story about a monster that lived under water banks. Also I wondered about some Kiowa paintings of such a water monster. I always thought they lived in oceans. But there is a story about this Kiowa man who claimed to have been taken to their underwater home; he later appeared back on land. Say he was a powerful medicine man but not so good-looking, and some people were afraid of him. Think they called him Tone-awh-k'oat [Tonakɔt] — Snapping or Rough Tailed Turtle. Seems he used his medicine the wrong way, which eventually killed him. Seems the story anyway.[14] Maybe a different version somewhere. I do know one thing tho, when I was a small guy and about to get in the water with others, I'd be leery about that dark water under a bank or tree. This was way before I heard the story. So maybe it was inherent. We'd tease each other about it. I also remembered a story Dad told me when I was a tot.

When Dad started a story, he always emphasized the fact that these were before the whiteman were here. They never heard of them (whitemen). Indians were considered wild and therefore had the senses that the animals had. Sorta like you feel or sense something's around but can't see, hear, or smell it. But you know it's there. I've seen it in animals when they get close to me but couldn't see hear or smell me. It's amazing to watch how they react as they get closer. I've had that feeling when hunting alone in the hills and mountains. Like I'm not alone, and something's watching me. And there usually is. I've seen deer and elk come within ten or fifteen feet of me before they sensed something just wasn't right. Those are the ones I didn't get because the brush was too thick for a shot, or they were so close that any movement on my part would blow the whole deal. When that close, do not look an animal in the eye.

But back to Dad's story. For whatever reason, sometimes a warrior would get separated from his party, or maybe he jus went out to "fast" for his medicine. Anyway, this young warrior seems to have got his directions mixed at night and lost his way. Warriors in that day ran most of the time to cover long distances. This young man ran a long way at night and was in need of some cold water. As he ran, he noticed a tree outline and soon a reflection from the moonlight on water. As he approached the water, he noticed the outline of a very high cliff on the opposite side bank. He reaches the water's edge and lays down to drink. But sensing something wasn't quite right, like he was not alone or being watched and, whatever it was, was not an animal. K'Ỹai (enemy)? Way out in nowhere or unfamiliar and wild country. Of course, these young Kiowa warriors are known for their bravery, but this one felt way out of the ordinary. He looked up and seen a figure not unlike a human (man) being outlined by the moon on the cliff across from him. He could barely make out some configurations on each side of its head, a sort of leafy curve.

And soon as he noticed it, it leaped into the air and dove off the cliff. When it leaped, he thought it was going for him, but the river was wide, so the warrior jumped up and back. While it was outlined in the moonlight when it jumped, he caught a slight glimpse of its feet, which were not like human feet but were by proportion somewhat larger and wider. It hit the water with a big splash and then silence. He stood there for some time to see or hear whatever was to surface. Nothing but silence though. Having enough of that and pretty much unnerved, he lit out in what he hoped to be the right direction to his people. When these stories are told, it's mostly with Kiowa words, which if you understood are so comical or seriously scary. I wish I could remember all of them. You'd think by hearing some of them, you'd think twice about going out alone. Some people really are afraid to do that. We'd tease them and say, "Aw, what are you scared of, nobody or nothing would want you anyway." You're too ornery, or you don't bathe anyway.

You know, I've been out on mostly hunting trips out in the mountains and hills, sometimes at night, but it seems I give those no thought. I probably know all the trails or other things about the areas within our five-mile radius at least. Even at night.

About owls Mom used to tell me, "They can't hurt you; they're just birds." So I'm okay with that. But she did tell a story about an owl one time that got me to thinking. And I did have an experience with owls a couple times. Not the ones I tried to hatch with a nite-lite. Or the one forgot and left in her corner wall clothes closet. Wooo! She used to be afraid to look in my dresser drawers or closet. Nothing. I yam what I yam!

I don't know if I mentioned this earlier, but I'll mention it again in case. Mom and her sister, Aunt Margaret Apayyat Methvin, were maybe around nine or ten years old and staying with their grandpa Odlepaugh about a mile west of Saddle Mountain Church. Odlepaugh and his wife, An-na-daw-mah [Kol-an-on-da-mah], or Ananthy to whiteman, raised Mom until their deaths. Aunt Margaret was there off and on, I guess, and Mom and her decided they wanted to walk to church. While walking and talking for about halfways there, when Mom remembered something about the pasture they were crossing. Mom remembered this mean bull that lived in that area. They both stopped and didn't know what to do, as they were scared and started to cry. Margaret asked Mom, "What are we going to do now; we're a long way from home and Grandpa can't hear us?" Mom said, "Naw, ahm bay-daw-t'sy." "You pray for us, Margaret." Well, Margaret put her hands together, then stopped and looked at Mom. Margaret said, "You pray. You're the one that was saved." Guess she meant Mom went to the altar one time to accept Jesus Christ as her savior or baptized. Lol!

Mom and her sister, Margaret, were just visiting and talking, I guess, when Mom asked Margaret, "What did you see in him to marry him?" They were talking about Margaret's husband, William Methvin, or Billy High, as he was better known around here. Margaret said, "Well, I thought he was handsome." Well, Mom bout went thru the floor in disbelief, as she didn't think Billy High was anything close to handsome. Mom said saw-pole-mah (you owl)! Owl word is used as a derogatory term, as Kiowa don't have curse words in vocabulary. Say what they want, they're sisters. Us kids thought it was funny, anyhow.

It wasn't a good feeling then or even now, but I was sorta aw dae (spoiled, pet, etc.). Mom expected me to succeed in whatever and thought out of all her kids, I was the bright one. Guess moms can tell or see something in their kids that others don't. She let me tag along with her most of the time she went somewhere. Thinking I was really going somewhere, I'd wind up at a sewing meeting! Pretty boring, but I wanted to go. Not just that tho. At times we'd go to

Gotebo to get some bote. There was a little slaughterhouse there. One time Clifton took me into that slaughterhouse. I didn't know what it was, but it stank. We sat on a bench to watch. There was a cow in this pen, and I didn't know what to expect. Rodeo? Lol! A man soon came in and walked right up to that poor cow and just shot him between the eyes. Man, that thing just dropped like he'd been sledgehammered. The man stuck this long metal rod down the cow's throat and pulled the cow outta the pen and started butchering. I thought it was scary and gross. But Clifton got a kick out of it. I said I wouldn't eat anything like that. Clifton said, "Well, starve then." But he did buy me a big red what was called a "delicious apple." Never had one like that. He asked me, "Think you can kill it?" Didn't know what he meant then. Meant could I eat the whole thing. I couldn't. Too big.

Got away from my aw-dae story. Mom would sometimes wake me early before the others and say to be quiet. I didn't know the first time what was going on. We'd quietly leave the house and get in the car and go. We'd (Dad and Mom) stop somewhere and eat breakfast. We'd either go to Wichita Falls, Texas, or Oklahoma City. Turns out she took me shopping. Clothes, shoes, etc. I remember this big building in Oklahoma City where we went first. A John A. Brown department store. I didn't think I deserved any of that. Whatever Mom had for me in life didn't quite turn out like that. She even planned my marriage to our preacher's daughter, which I didn't know about. Her and the preacher's wife had it planned. I didn't know about that until years later when my sister, Lavena, told me. I didn't even know that girl that well. We never talked.

### November 2019 Narrative

I'm going to go back to our young days and our crew in the country and a few escapades. There would be really too many to write the stories. Wish I could write them all. Up at Uncle Cecil Horse's house was another house on the north side of us, where my brother, John Tsatoke, lived with his family. Later, brother-in-law Vic Rivera and Stella and family lived there. Sometime in the fifties my sister Evelyn Tsatoke Bread and crew moved into Uncle Cecil's house. She had five sons, Charles Jr., known to us as "Tooter"; Jimmy; Donald, or "Jinxy"; Jerry; and Gene, in that order. They lived in Lawton before that and were considered "city boys" to us. They liked it out there and caught on to our style. They liked to fish, swim, hike, and hunt, but I had to show them how to fish, hunt, and of course how to shoot a rifle and the safety and maintenance thereof. Took them awhile for that but were willing to learn and, man, did we have a time of it. I don't think they took a rifle too serious or how to hunt but liked the adventure of it. I had to show them the outdoors way. Years later they'd say I was their Danial [Daniel] Boone. The Cody girls said I was their Tarzan.

On one of our hunting trips past the old Jim Tracey Ranch into the forested canyons about one and a half miles ssw of our place, I knocked down a deer and here goes. After the shot we all took to the brushy hillside to hide, as the hired hand at the ranch probably heard it. We didn't have permission to be in there, from him anyway. Well, sure enough, I heard his old Jeep start up. He had two metal gates to open, so I knew where he'd be. Hidden in the brushy hills, I got a glimpse of him passing by. He went to the end of the road and waited and listened. After about thirty or forty minutes he started back. After I heard the second gate close and a little later his Jeep door shut, I made my move and gave a quail whistle twice. The lesser "bawanas" came out of the leaves. I went to where I last saw the deer fall in a dry creek bed. I had covered him with leaves to hide him. Well, he wasn't where I covered him. Somebody said, "Look." About fifteen yards from that covered place there he (deer) stood, scared me. I thought he was dead. He started to run but couldn't get going. I didn't want to shoot again because the shot would bring back the hired hand.

The deer was making slow strides down the creek bed. Oh man, what to do. Telling those guys not to make any kinda noise like hollering, yelling, so I cowboyed up and tried bulldogging him. Them things is tuff. I finally got my hatchet, conk him in the head, and dead. All the while listening for that Jeep to start up. After I slew him we drug him into the brush and hid again and waited another thirty minutes. After we figured all was clear, we stood around and wondered how to carry him, as we were going to have to go way around the way we came in, so as not to be seen or heard. That creek ran right below his ranch, and we'd have to sneak by or go up another route. Anyway, while standing there "thinkin," hero, Tooter, Charles Bread Jr., said, "I got him," and squatted down and told us to load the deer across his shoulders, him being the biggest and wanted to "star." His brother, Jimmy, said, "Okay, Danial Boone." So we load the deer across his shoulders and help him up a little bit. So here we go toward the long way around. I wondered about this but didn't say anything. We go about ten yards and I hear "Danial Boone" start to sing out, "Oh s — t! Oh s — t!" I look back, and "Mr. Boone" is starting to take quick short steps forward while leaning forward. He quickens his steps and, for crying out loud, our hero Danial Boone falls forward flat on his face! Lol! Deer laying across his head. "Mr. Boone" cusses, trying to be quiet. "Get this damn thing offa me." We just stand there trying to be quiet while cracking up. Oh! Oh man. Mr. Boone is whining? Finally, his brother, Jimmy, says, "Okay Danial Boone." Lol!

I suggest we cut a stout pole to put between the front and back legs, tied at the ankles to carry by two men. They say, good idea. Jimmy wants to tote the front pole, and Spi, a.k.a. Herman Methvin, bro, has the back pole. We go about fifty yards when Jimmy Bread just throws his front end down and hollers, "I ain't carrying that damn thing no more." Tooter says, "What's the matter? You wanted to." Jimmy says, "I don't care, that damn thing keeps poking his nose into my bisuness!" Ha, ha! Oh man! Turns out the deer's head was tied with the head forward and behind Jimmy about two feet off the ground when walking that way, the head swings forward and back; turns out, when the head swings forward, its nose was poking into Jimmy's business (zile) (buns), Har-de-har! So we just tied its head up. Perks you up when you're tired.

Another time, same area, we were hunting squirrels when one runs up this big pecan tree. About six or seven feet from the main trunk of the tree, the squirrel runs into a hole in the limb away from the main trunk. Now Tooter seen me do this before when that happens, just not how he did it. I just climb to the hole and chop around the hole to enlarge it, so as to get my hand into it. If the hole is kinda roomy, it's not a good idea to reach in, as the squirrel has room to turn around and bite. And they will bite. I warned Tooter about it. If the hole is sorta tight where the squirrel is, then you're safe as he can't turn around. You just slide your hand along where you can grab a leg or two and slowly pull. When you get him almost out, you give him a hard yank and jerk him out while in the same motion, bash the head against the tree trunk so as not to give him a chance to bite.

So Tooter says, "I'll get 'em!" He climbs the tree to about twelve feet off the [ground] and scoots out onto the limb with the hole. I see right away what may or is gonna happen, but "Mr. Guitar-Zan" is too busy stealing the show. Below and nailed to the tree as a corner post is an old "hog wire" fence about four-feet high. Oh, get this! The Danial Boone now turned hatchet man starts to choppin around the limb, supposedly to enlarge the hole. Note. The hole is between him and the tree. He's chopping between him and the tree. Yep! The limb breaks and down comes the "Junior Woodchuck." He steals the show! What a way to go! And he hits that old "hog wire" fence and cuts his hand pretty bad and bleeds a lot. The men are in shock and scared; we're a ways from home. I doctor him with some fresh moss and a lil watercress, which bites a little, and some mud. A bandage from his T-shirt, some cold biscuits, and spring water gets him ready for another episode in the wilds of the Tracey Ranch and other parts of the area.

We had our way of communication when we wanted to know the whereabouts of the other party we are to meet. At a point in a vee to where we're headed. We'd put our fingers together and cup our hands together and clasp them together. Usually the right hand over the left, between the thumb and index finger of the left palm. Bring our thumbs together and bend them inward. Leave bowl-like chamber between the palms. With our thumb's knuckles bent, we'd blow through them. It took some practice to make a whistling sound. We needed to make a good seal with the cupping of hands. When you got it right, it made a good hollow whistling sound that carried a good way off. By lifting the left palm fingers a little while blowing and squeezing, fingers cupped, it made a higher-pitched sound. You could also, while blowing, lift your left palm fingers a little at a time or flutter them, opening and closing the left palm for different tones, hollow or shrill. We'd copy the others sound like a ten-four. We'd know how far we were from each other.

If we happen to be out at night, we made the owl sound. Which brings to mind a friend or companion of mine at the time. My brothers, James, Spi Methvin, or Snake Methvin were going fishing one evening about a mile and half east of our place in the country. I told my companion, a Pat Hollingshead, who is half-Comanche and half-white, to take us out there and come back for us about ten that night. This Mrs. Hollingshead claimed to be the outdoors type, having grew up on a farm northeast of Apache.

James and I were very familiar with the areas surrounding our old home place. We knew where every trail, fence, creek banks, etc. were. Even in total darkness. She lets us off, and we go opposite directions to fish the creek. I told Pat to pick us up at the same place. She let us off. We timed it to be there at the same place. So, when we were done with our fishing, it was dark. We couldn't see each other but knew just about where the other was. We were about seventy-five yards from the pickup place and could just barely make out Pat's car. She made it. I could see her silhouette, as I knew James could. I made the owl sound and stopped. James did the same, I guess. So we just stayed where we were. We watched Pat walking back and forth, trying to see if we were coming. She starts walking faster and really looking around. About to panic? So I made a low owl sound. She stops pacing, lifts her head, looks to the heavens, and lets out a loud scary, hootie hoot! Hootie hoot? Oh, I and James bout blew a gasket cracking up. But you know? She said she knew where we were all that time and wasn't scared. Yeah, right. Said she was communicating with the saw-poles (owls). Didn't know she could talk with owls. Yo! A real saw-pole-mah? (Owl Woman?) Yo! "Yo" is NDN for scary or scared.

About twenty years ago I told Pat to take me out to the country to fish and to come get me later. It was about 4:00 p.m. when I got off, about one and a quarter mile east of our place. As I said earlier, I know my way around out there, even at night. Told her to pick me up at our old place out there at 10:00 that night. I know she wanted to ask me how I was gonna see to get around out there, but she didn't ask. I had a mess of fish and walked to our old place. I squatted down in the creek, found a flat rock, and started fileting the fish. Having got there about 9:00 p.m. While cleaning fish, I noticed it was awful quiet. All I could hear was a little gurgle of the water running and the little noise I made. After a few minutes I just squatted to rest a bit. It was so quiet but good because, if she was coming, I'd hear her car.

Well, the minute I stopped, I 'bout came unglued. I didn't hear a sound like that before. Suddenly, and I mean suddenly, there, right above my right shoulder, loud talking-barking, popping-almost scream sounded off! What I mean, it startled the hell outta me! All of a sudden it sounded. I didn't know how long it was there or hear it fly up, but the damn thing got to me and made me so damned mad 'cause it scared me. And I don't scare like that. I cussed him out and cracked up. Damn you. You scared me. You blankety blank, I thought, it was probably cracking up too. But I did get a good laugh out of it. Their feathers are so soft you don't hear them fly. Was it the "Owl Woman," Pat? ☺

Back to the country a bit. The driveway from the road, now Highway 58, was always bad after a good rain, and we and others usually got cars stuck. When it was too muddy, Dad would just park the car by the mailbox there until it dried enough to drive down.

We'd have to walk down to the house and carry what we needed. Groceries, etc. you got muddy alright, plus if you slipped and fell. The driveway from the road up there was right at three hundred yards. We also waited and caught the school bus up there. Rain, sleet, or snow. Years ago our house was up there by the road, but Grandpa moved it down to the creek, so as to have better access to water.

Across the creek was where the dance ground and baseball field were. A nice pasture for that. On the east side of the pasture was a fence with gate that led to the gravel road, quarter mile north of the house. Well, when the road was muddy, Dad drove around to the gate and across the pasture to the east side of the creek. We walked and waded the creek with our goods. The pasture grass was easy to drive on, and you didn't get muddy or stuck. But . . . it, where the car was parked to the house, was a good hundred yards or little more down to the creek, flooded most times, and up a sorta steep slope to the house.

Dad would carry us across sometimes when the water was too swift or deep. Plus, everything else we needed. He'd make several trips sometimes. He even carried Mom across at times. We thought that kinda funny or something, but we dared not say anything. But I wonder what they thought. ☺ I remember Brother Spi one time got swept away trying to show off and cross. He was flailing away and going fast. I chased him around a couple bends in the creek, but he was having a time through the brush. Lol! O man. He was testifying to beat the Holiness Band drum! And when I thought he might be gone, I spied a willow limb hanging just over the water ahead of him and hollered to him to grab it and hang on. He grabbed it just about the time I reached the bank. There he hung on until I could get a hold and pull him out. I could sense his face going around the bend. Was kinda funny at first. Guess I cudda said I grabbed a grapevine and swung out after him.

The road up to the highway was bordered on the north by a wheat field. It was higher than our road at the time, so there was a bank on the north side of the road. In the winters the wind, sleet, and snow swept across the barren wheat field, and it was cold and windy. We'd squat down against the bank for a windbreak, which was about three to three and a half feet high. We got rained on, of course. I'd think that we were like cotton-tailed rabbits huddled against the scant windbreak. The bus driver was afraid of getting stuck or sliding into the creek where the road bended by the creek. Anyway, Dad came up with one of his ideas one day. He built a shelter on skids and drug it up to the road. Wow! We had a good shelter with peep holes to watch for the bus. Even had seats. The white kids thought it was funny because it looked like a kinda large outhouse. Served its purpose well though.

I think we got our first TV in 1956. *Mickey Mouse Club* and Walt Disney were popular, as was the *Ed Sullivan Show*. Of course, Mom liked *Queen for a Day*, which I figured was just a phony. *Bonanza* and *Dragnet*. We didn't have color TV at the time. Before that the only TV around was two and a half miles north at Uncle Barney and Aunt Fern Adahkobo Davis's house. Men in the Indian families in the area, including us, would converge at Uncle Barney's house for the Wednesday and Friday night fights. That was something to us, even though it was crowded and a twelve- or fourteen-inch TV. But "The Cavalcade of Sports is on the air" there. Gillette razor blades, foamy shaving-cream advertising. Boy, I got to see Joe Louis, Archie Moore, Jersey Joe Walcott, Sugar Robinson, Kid Savilan [Gavilán], Rocky Marciano, Carmen Basiclo [Basilio], and all the rest of the great ones of that era. Even though you got only three or four channels, it didn't matter. Long as you had "Game on!" No Coke or popcorn, a lotta "Down in front, can't see through muddy water."

I can't say that I believe in ghosts, but some things make me think. As said, I've hunted those hills of our mountains around there alone many times and know just about all the different bird and animal sounds or silhouettes. Whether it's wild or domestic, just by its stance, movement, or run. To the south of our place and a half mile past the old gravel road that turns back east by Jim Tracey Ranch, it starts to get rugged country. I was starting my deer hunt there at a creek below a long grade toward the top of a mountain. I was going to circle around the area downwind to hunt deer. There was a fence line toward the top. Well, about halfway up there I had this little feeling like I wasn't alone in that wild place. Like something was watching me. I'd stop, listen, and slowly turn and look around to where I passed. I couldn't hear or see anything out of the ordinary and not too windy. I had my trusty .30-30 Winchester lever-action with 170 grain bullets. It held seven rounds if you had one chambered. I stopped twice more and sat. I scrutinized that area for a long time. Fence line, few brush, and some pasture. Still nothing, but the feeling didn't go away. So I started up again, took a few steps, stopped, and turned around quick-like. It was about 250 yards below me. Whatever. Thought I saw something dark that didn't fit. I plopped down and "opened up" toward whatever. Seemed outta place to me. I don't know. I didn't want to go look, so I circled way around on the way back and checked the area. No sign. Was there a small gulley hidden in the grass? That was around 1972. There are now, but I hadn't heard or seen wild hogs out there when I was out there that time. I've had deer parallel me while I walked and had that feeling when I didn't notice them. They learn your movements and are probably watching you; they're not too dumb. They know every inch of their area and every escape route.

Was down the creek at our old place, hunting elk. I did everything right so far. I didn't see it, but was sure I was within fifty yards of this big bull. After coming up downwind and, I figured, behind him as they lay with their [noses] to the wind. I snuck up the area where I figured he'd lay, in a jumbled mess of flooded-up limbs. I sat there and with binoculars gazed that area. Hard to tell, but I was sure he was there. I was gonna sit down on this log await 'til he moved or stood. I did not look to see for a clear shot. Just sat down on this small log. As I sat quietly down, I had sat on a vine of thorns. Ow! No, I didn't holler, tho it hurt. I eased up and away a few inches, and, yes, a half-inch thick, dry limb made a little crack, not something loud, but that bull heard it, exactly where I thought he was. He was up and melted into the brush. Busted limb, busted hunt. That is hunting.

I heard from Dad and some others about Grandpa (James "Kiowa" Jim). I don't know the year(s) that Grandpa took in some kong-ghe-ohns, Blacks. Dad said one day a couple with a son and daughter, I think, were traveling by in a wagon and team and stopped to ask for water. Guess they visited for a while, then Grandpa ask them where they were going. The Black man answered, "Don't know, we jus going." After resting a bit they said they need to get on down the road, as it was late in the day. But Grandpa told them get down and spend the night, as it was late.

The next day Grandpa, knowing these people didn't have a place to go, invited them to just stay on, and he'd find work for them around the ranch. He cleaned out the chicken house, and that's where they stayed until I don't know when. They had a son about Dad's age named Eugene. I don't know his mother or father's names. Or how long they stayed there. Seemed like they had a young daughter also.

East of the house and across the creek about a quarter mile is a small hill. On that hill I think are three graves, which are probably lost to sight, but I remember one time Melissa and I went to look for the grave site. We were young, but I do remember seeing evidence of a grave site. A few stones and small indentations in the ground. I think there were three. Think Dad agreed on three. My sister, Vivian Tsatoke Komardly, told me of her and Grandma was the elder buried there. And I think the little Black girl from that family Grandpa invited to stay. I don't know, but sister Lisa Tongkeamha LaBrada and Vivian told me the grandmother's name is "Ho-aun-tah-le," "Trail Boy." That I heard of and seen in genealogy book in the Lawton library. These old names are sometimes hard to decipher. The meaning may not be in the spelling or the pronunciation. It gets deep. The Black family must have stayed for a while, as Dad told me; the Black boy learned and spoke the Kiowa language, as did his parents. Guess they also picked up Kiowa ways.

Those Kiowa boys would pull pranks on Eugene, the Black boy.

Grandpa usually had a big "blow out" Fourth of July celebration there. One Fourth, Eugene's mom got him a brand-new pair of coveralls to wear that day. He was proud of them; he'd run around those men, showing off his new coveralls. The Horse boys, Geiontys, Kaulays, and others, in those days they had these big red firecrackers, about two and a half inches long. Well, this Eugene comes to where these guys were sitting to show off. Just dancing and prancing around. Well, while Eugene was showing off, one of those guys lights one of those big red ones and slips it into Eugene's hip pocket. Wham! He jumps up, hollers, and heads for the creek with hip pocket hanging and flapping around. Fixed his little red wagon. Those guys got another kinda kick out of it, I guess. Cruel? Cold blooded? Gotta be tough, I guess.

Years later Dad said he was walking down an off street by an auto garage [in Lawton]. The mechanic hollers, "Hey, Saw-pole P'ah-bee" [Owl Brother]. It was Eugene of the day's past. Talked of the old days, Dad said. That part of land across the creek where the graves are was sold some time back. I'm sure the graves are still there with their stories.

In the late 1980s I and friend Pat Hollingshead came for something in Carnegie. I think it was late spring, as the weather was nice. We had two sleeping bags and decide to "ruff it" and sleep out by the water's edge down the creek. There were no powwows going on around there. I built a fire, and we talked 'til we got sleepy. I didn't know what it was when I felt something poking the side of my chest. Kinda sharp. Then I heard Pat whisper, "You awake?" Well, I said I was. She said, "You hear that?" Well, I did hear it before she poked me. "Yes," I said. I thought it was just me that heard it. It was so faint one could barely hear it. I thought maybe an old windmill but knew there wasn't any in that area. Now I've heard this before but didn't tell anybody. Only about twice before that. I knew what it sounded like but didn't tell her, so I asked her what it sounded like to her. She said, "Sounds like somebody singing like at a powwow." I was surprised she said that because that's what it sounded like to me.

So I told her it was just Grandpa and his powwow because we were almost next to it. Melissa and Pam also told me they heard it. That's why I feel secure and at peace when I'm out there for a few days. The old ones are still here and glad I visit there. They know. Sometimes I camp out at our old place to find peace of mind and reminisce. I fish some of the old places that are left. You can hardly tell where a house and relatives used to live. Indian churches around the area had men and women softball teams. Saddle Mountain, Rainy Mountain, Cache Creek, Boone, Cedar Creek, Samone, Hog Creek, Mountain Scott Kiowa were some of them. Both Baptist and Methodist. There was always a game going on somewhere. Especially on weekends. We had a baseball diamond, as the women played softball. Seems like it was in the middle fifties that fast-pitch softball showed up. Baseball and softball were the big thing then. Seemed like the only thing in entertainment. Our whole family played the game.

I remember going to the Bointy's, Fritz Kaulay's, Albert Cody's, Jasper Hokeah's, where the women would visit, and the men played dominoes, which I did not understand at the time. I thought they were trying to figure out how to make something with the dominoes, a pattern of some kind. I was pretty young, and adults were a puzzle. We kids had our games, of which some were learned from others. Of course, today you won't see them played anymore. Too busy with their phones and electric toys, especially the Facebook. They are lost to the real world. Even families are ignored for these things. Pushed God completely out. And they wonder what's wrong with them and their own families. Why do they have troubles? They've created idols that can't and won't do anything for them. It won't, says them. Some will disagree, but to me the old days were the best. Things were slower and simpler. We had more time for family and closeness of family and ate real food. We weren't pushed to buy something that would be junk in a few weeks. Or somebody's getting scammed every minute.

I remember going to town (Carnegie) a couple of times on a wagon and team. Seemed like it took most of the morning. The road was gravel and dirt then. It was slow, I guess, but we didn't mind. Grandma would wrap me in a blanket, but I didn't like that. I wanted to see the country. Sometimes we'd jump off the wagon and run alongside it. It was fun until we got hollered at too much. They were afraid we'd get run over. The dog would follow for a while.

There were a lot of sunflowers by the side of the road. They just stood and watched you go by. Grandma called them "Ho-sawm," "Road Watchers." One time our car got stuck in mud on the dirt road up to the highway, and after a time Dad got pretty mad. He'd get out and dig the mud away and put grass or anything else in front of the wheel(s) that was spinning, for traction. We'd get out and help push. We'd get sprayed with mud but didn't mind. Well, Dad gets out of the car and "took it out" on the nearest sunflowers. He imagined them just standing there watching and maybe smiling at him, so he gets mad, starts sockin' them around. You didn't hear a peep out of us. By that time we were none too clean but on our way to town. Guess Dad got over his mad 'cause, by the time we got to Dirty Shame, he was singing. Mom sorta smiled, and we let our breath out.

Compared to now, Carnegie was a pretty large town. To us anyway. It was another world to us kids. In the late forties and fifties, there were a lot of stores and things to do. The stores stayed open late to accommodate the farm and ranch workers. I'm talking about ten or eleven closings for some stores like cafés, dry goods and gas stations, and three cotton gins that I remember. And yes, three dry goods stores. JCPenney, the Dixie Store being the largest. A smaller Goodman's dry goods and the smaller one. Three grocery stores and four or five smaller neighborhood groceries. Two movie theaters, the Nu-Show and Liberty Theatre, which is still operating today. Friday, Saturday, and Sunday and afternoon matinees, with a later and different movie. The late one was called "Preview." The Saturday show always had a serial that would end in "to be continued next week." One serial went on and on, but if you wanted to see what happened to your hero, villain, or damsel in distress, you had to find more empty pop bottles to sell, or, though not to sound like whining, you asked your dad or mom; usually you asked your mom first, who promptly told you to ask your dad, who told you the same thing. As Saturday neared, you got real brave and asked or hunt empty pop bottles, which sold for two cents a bottle, no cracks in them. You just had to find out what happened next at Saturday's continued series chapter. Ten cents for movie, five cents for an RC Cola real bottle of pop and a bag of Tom's salted peanuts, which you poured into your bottle of pop. If you had enough, you got a bag of popcorn for five cents. Twenty cents made you rich. I remember getting a quarter for the first time and didn't know what it was. A big nickel? My city-slicker brothers knew, though, and I had, all at once, a bunch of p'ah-bees (brothers). I was pretty popular right off.

The Goodman's dry goods store was owned by a Jew, whatever that was. He'd try to sell you anything or everything, even if it didn't fit. Frank (Jughead) would say, "Jes thee feat, for that $1.98." Mr. Goodman would have you try on a shirt, coat, or jacket. If it was too big, and you told him so, he'd pull on the back of it to take up the front slack and announce "jus thee feat for the $1.98." I don't know if that worked for him or not. Likely not, he didn't seem to have too much business.

JCPenney and the Dixie Store is where I noticed the way payments were made. They both had upper and lower floors. After a purchase and you had change coming, you had to wait a bit. The salesperson would put the money and the sales slip in a three- or four-inch bronze or copper tube that snaked its way to the upper floor. In a little while the change and receipt came back down the tube, which she opened for your change. As a kid, I thought, where did my money go. I didn't trust that thing. Every purchase was wrapped in a plain-spun, coarse-paper wrap, which was on a big spool by the counter. A thin, stout cord was used to wrap the whole thing. I used them for my fishing line. Today you buy something, you get third degreed. Cash, card, pho[ne] #, address, etc. Can't just buy something.

On the east end of Carnegie Main Street was a big ice plant. They sold twenty-five-, fifty-, seventy-five-, or hundred-pound blocks of ice for the home icebox, plus ice cream. Brother Spi and I would go there and get a free ice cream sometimes. His dad, Uncle Billy High, worked there. Next to it, on the north side, was the VFW Hall, with a pool hall and domino parlor beneath it in a basement-type large room. It had two eight-ball tables and two snooker tables, I think. Mom didn't like us hanging out there, but it was cool in the summer. Upstairs in the VWF part is where benefit powwows were held on weekends. That was around 1958. Before the Gourd Dance came back around. The last dance I know of held there was 1960, when I was in the service.

Also, at the east end of Main Street was a big Kelley's Grocery store. Southside and behind the grocery was an alley and a big wooden water tank for the nearby railroad depot. And a warehouse that had benches on the east side by the water tank. That's where most of the Indian families sat and visited after shopping or just to wait for their kids to get out of the movies. Their horses and wagons were hitched to the water-tower supports. It was cool there, and the water tower leaked quite a bit. The horses and us kids liked that. If you were looking for someone, they'd say, "Look backa' Kelley's." Another family gathering place was right across and south of the Liberty Theatre. East side of a large hardware store. There was a large space there, and by the sidewalk was a small cart or building that sold snow-cones and popcorn by a man we called "Pop-Corn Mack."

I knew of three beer joints in town. Two on Main, and one two blocks south of the flagpole on Main. Three two-story hotels, a taxi-cab stand. Two beer joints on southeast edge of town by Highway 9. I knew a time when Indians had to drink in the back of the bar. One on the southeast edge was partitioned to Indians. There were three auto dealerships. A Kelley Ford, Gibson Pontiac, and a Bolin Chevrolet. Plus about three hardware stores. Four cafés and about nine or ten gas stations, plus three Dairy Queens. So there were some things to do on Saturdays when you got to town.

At different times these cowboy stars would be in town to promote their movies. Johnny Mack Brown, Hopalong Cassidy, Gene Autry, Roy Rogers, Tim Holt, and Lash LaRue. I even got to ride on a stagecoach with Hopalong Cassidy. Yes, they were the real deal. People wondered what they seen in Carnegie. Why they chose Carnegie. I remember Dad saying, while working the big cattle ranch of Jim Tracey, south of us about a mile and half, a whiteman showed up looking to buy some cattle while riding along. Turns out this man was Dale Roberton [Robertson], the movie-star cowboy. I asked Dad, did you "draw down on him?" That was some of Carnegie back in the day.

## December 2019 Narrative

I talked a little about music types come and go, as do fads. But I'm a die-hard for old-time country! Rhythm and blues of the 1950s. We had our styles of dress, clothing, dance, music, etc. If you didn't dress the style, you weren't hip or cool, as in "Cat-Man." You were a "Cat-Man" if dressed in the style of the fifties. The trousers were usually black denim with "pegged," narrow at the ankle. Shoes were usually black-laced wing tipped or with white bucks. Colors were black and white. You wore a thin, white belt. Then pink shirts with little black stitching. Hair styles were "ducktail," if you could manage it. Sometimes the hair would be a kind of "flattop" and combed back sides into a "ducktail." We used this hair grease we called "coon grease," which held your hair in place.[15] If too much was used, you had a shiny forehead and greasy ear tips. The hair dressings were Tuxedo Club, Royal Crown, and Three Flowers, which are still around today. But your head stood out after the '49. Everybody wore Levi jeans. Now some of the kids wore them low at the belt and would slit the seam on the outside of the cuff, about six to eight inches up. Or without belt loops. Of course, if Mom seen me do that, she sure would have a lot to say. Our dance was mostly "bop" with some jitterbuggin. And slang! Too many to mention. Some that we used were cat (guy), bread (money), wheels (car), heat (cops), what's shakin' (happenin'), tore up (drunk).

Towns like Carnegie, Fort Cobb, Anadarko, or Apache would have a teen dance (bop-hop) on a Friday or Saturday nite. Our gathering place in Carnegie was a little café called "The Chili Bowl." We'd go there to chat, drink Cokes, RC Cola and play the jukebox. Speaking of slang, it was during the Indian Fair, and we friends, or p'ah-bees (brothers), would gather to make our rounds at the fairgrounds. We were coming from town, Anadarko; my crew came by our camp to get me to go with them to the "grounds." There was a lot of family at our camp eating supper at this time. As I started to leave the large eating shade with them, I said, "Wait, I forgot something." So they stood there. I called Mom aside and asked her, "Mom, you got any bread?" She just looked at me and said, "Didn't you eat?" Oh, those guys just about busted a gut laughing. I meant money. Everybody heard. I told her what I meant. She said, "Why didn't you say so?" I said I did. She said, "You talk goofy." No man, we're cool!

Or the time one summer when we're leaving Anadarko, I was sitting in the front between Mom and Dad, as we had a carload. Anyway, as we passed the curve, I saw this skunk, "highway patrol," pull out behind us. Thinking Dad seen him too, I didn't say anything. Well, after following us for a while, I told Dad, "Hey man, the heat's on." You know, Dad reaches down to the car-heater knob and says, "No, it's not on; it's off." Oh man. The patrolman then turns on his top light and makes a "woop" sound. Dad said, "Why don't you tell me you saw him?" I said, "I did." I said the heat's on. And Mom sounds off again about my kinda talk. Ain't nothing shaking here but leaves on the trees. Gotta be cool, daddi-o!

We kids looked forward to going to the American Indian Exposition, Indian Fair to us. We didn't especially like loading or unloading our camping stuff though. About week or two before, we'd have to cut and make some tent poles and some stakes (t'hom-t'ol). T'hom-t'ol and poles were from chinaberry trees. T'hom-t'ol were about a foot long. We skinned the bark from them and sharpened to a good point. A notch was cut near the top to loop the rope around. That was work for us. About a mile west of our place was a grove of the trees about three to five inches in diameter. They were clustered, and when you drove by and glanced [at] them, they looked [like] they were dancing. These lower bare parts. That's why Dad called them "dancing trees."

I barely remember going to the fair by wagon and team. It was slow, but I had a fun time riding on a mattress in the wagon. The wagon was one of the old, green, government-issue army GI type. We'd stop on the way by a creek to water the horses and eat a snack. Ke-taw-p, dried meat, or salt pork bacon and biscuit sandwich. Grandma usually has her dried apricots in her "Indian purse," a scarf tied in many knots and wore on her sash or belt. We took the Alden to Broxton to Stecker Road. By that road we would come out even with the now Anadarko Airport. Right south of the airport and on a little rise was Grandpa Enos Smokey's place. He had an old cast-iron water pump with a long pump handle. We used his water at our camp because, as everybody around there knew about Anadarko. It was gypey [gypsum-like texture] and bad tasting. Also gave you "bote-kope," stomach trouble, and the runs if you didn't live in 'Darko. It was bad for you. Dad would have about four or five of those old metal ten-gallon or so cream cans, which he filled. We used that water during the fair. The 'Darko people must have had a different kind of gut.

We usually camped on the south side of the south campground and by a fence, so the gawkers couldn't pass our camp on the south side and kick up the dust on us. A week before the Expo started is when we put up our camp and a few furnishings. The Sunday or Saturday before things started, we moved the rest of stuff in. The following Monday was the parade day. Mom would have me stay and watch things at the camp after the first load. I had food and some money to last me, which was about four days. I was okay with that because they'd have a big Indian softball tournament three days before the Expo started. Parade day was when Mom brought out new clothes for us kids. Dad cut our hair, and we showered at the Christian Center. We were shined up. Even our foreheads shone with hair oil.

After the parade more people headed for the big grandstand for the afternoon program. There was the Navajo Nation tribal band from Window Rock, Arizona, local citizen band, and Indian-owned horse races. At the intervals tribal dancers came out, and the grandstand would be packed. Popcorn, soda, peanut, and snow-cone caterers roamed the stands, hollering and selling their wares. It was quite a sight and feeling. A big carnival and midway was right behind the grandstand with food booths below it. At night we would sit at the top seating of the grandstand and watch the rides and people.

For three nights a pageant was presented, while other nights were intertribal dancing with contesting took place on Thursday and Friday nights. World champions were crowned. These were from the Kiowa, Comanche, Apache, Cheyenne, Arapaho, Ponca, Otoe, Osage, Caddo, Wichita, Delaware, and other visiting tribes. There was a partially built exhibit building that had just the cinder-block walls and concrete floor. A DJ was set up with our music and danced into the night. There was also an old exhibit building we called "the Barn" that was our dance hall.

One evening Gerald Horse, Perry Horse, and Herb Redbird and I were standing by the gate to the south campground about the time when the dancers for the night's program were walking toward the grandstand to dance. Well, along comes this dressed-up War Dancer with war paint on. This dancer got a hold of my hand and said, "Walk me to the grandstand." I tried to pull my hand away, but the grip was firm. My p'ah-bees just got quiet. Lol! This War Dancer spoke in my ear and said, "It's me," in a feminine voice. Lol! It was a Cheyenne girlfriend, but I didn't know she was a War Dancer. Anyway, as we walked off, I could hear one of my p'ah-bees say, "Dang, p'ah-bee's got a dude!" I don't know if they knew who she was. After the night's program people just hung around the grandstand watching the crowd. About midnight here come the '49ers. And it was a '49.[16] Sometimes two '49s were going on, plus a couple stomp-dance groups; those were the last real '49s of the 1950s. They danced for real and sang all night with no cops to bother. No holds barred. Enter at your own risk. There was a place at the time called "Snake Pit," where a mighty '49 took place also. About a half mile west of nowadays Wal-Mart. Right north of the airport curve going west. An old road led to a dead end. I was about fourteen or fifteen when my bunch decided to check it out. One night in 2002 I decided to go check out the Indian Fair in 'Darko. I was sitting with my older p'ah-bee, Ernie Keahbone, under a little canopy outside the exhibit hall. We were talking about the old Indian Fairs and friends and how things used to be. The announcer at the grandstand was going over the night's program. We never heard of one before, but there was to be a '49 contest that night. Ernie said, "'49 contest?" They need to go to "Snake Pit." Heck, there ain't no '49 contest. Leave it to today's kids to do something maw-bay'nh. Dumb. Today they try to have an Indian Fair, but it's always a bust.

Everybody wants to be chief with no knowledge of how to go about it. It's the same in tribal governments or other tribal organizations. No education or experience, but the desire to be seen and heard. These kinds are the ones who know deep down they don't really amount to much, so they try and do put themselves in position(s) to be heard and seen. For example, a short guy or wannabe, someone who feels inferior, may drive a big rig, eighteen-wheeler, or [be] a cop. They will just take it upon themselves that they should be the ones to do such and such. People even think that a family name is all that is required to justify the position. When I hear someone say their family is more traditional and cultural than other families, the same tribe, I feel so sorry for them. It's also comical, like "surely you jest." But you'll hear it and see it. It makes me wince, and I'll make a note to pray for them. "Forgive them. For they know not what they do."

If you claim to believe in the "one and only God," you should know that He created us all equal. There is "no one" better than the other. Not in God's world anyway. Envy leads to jealousy, dislike, and hate. You know or don't know that person. You are close kin to that person or friends, yet something about that person usually causes envy to rear its ugly head, which brings on all the other bad things. No matter what, it's there and all over the world. Some call envy "the Green Monster." Green with envy! It's said, "We all have skeletons in our closets." It affects everything and everybody. By and large, I myself am no way a saint. I have a long ways to go. Yet I know that deep down I will never graduate. It was never meant to be. "In this world you will always have trouble, but take heart! I have overcome the world." John 33:16. To me it means "overcome the world—our, my sins." He died for me. Yes, even me. He took my sins with Him in death. I believe Jesus was crucified, died, was resurrected on the third day, and lives. When He rose, on the third day, He rose and was clean of our sins so that we can live. To live, really live, is to be free of sin. If I doubt that He died for you and I, then I have failed and feel I just wasted His time on me. But He caused the sun to waken me to yet another day. No matter how cloudy or bad the morning, His sun still shines through. Little did I know that He still has something for me to do. I will try not to waste His time on myself. I will read His word and be still before Him. I will give Him all my attention in the time He has provided for me. I know He already knows what my day will be like. He knew even before I was born. He waits for me while I pray and meditate on His word. He just wants me to talk to Him first. As in all things, put God's word first. For He is a jealous God and is ahead of everything else. I always state the fact that, if we don't put God first in everything, we have nothing and are nothing.

He (God) know all the fears, doubts, and troubles you want to take up first thing on awakening. Do not do that, no matter how urgent, bad, or anything else. Only God matters right now. We are full of excuses and made-up or lame justifications to do what we want to do. Be still and know that I am God. Psalm 46:10. "For your thoughts are not my thoughts, neither are your ways my ways." Isaiah 55:8.

The first thing I do when God wakes me is reach for my spiritual readings. *Upper Room, Jesus Calling, My Time with God,* and my ever-present AA *Twenty Four Hours a Day* and the Bible scriptures that ensue. After reading I will meditate on the scriptures I read. I think about all the people I can, and they're still here or maybe gone on. Every one of them had something to do with my life or still do. Maybe some memories are bad, but that doesn't matter now. I will see them in my mind and pray for them. Every day a different set of people will come to mind. I nearly always have a Kiowa hymn going on in my mind. Sometimes an English hymn. That tells me God is always with or near me. Joshua 1:5. "I will never leave you or forsake you."

Don't worry about what went wrong or bad the day before. That was yesterday, and it's gone forever. You cannot undo yesterday. Don't try to. You cannot go forward while looking back and don't stop to examine the place where you fell. Yesterday, with all its ills, is gone with the wind, and if you live today with God, you will see a tomorrow with God; there is always a tomorrow. And God does not or cannot lie. We all fall short of the goal God set for us, but He doesn't want us to quit.

I'll always remember back in the old Saddle Mountain Church days. Sundays, revivals, Christmas, and Bible schools. The old people prayed so hard and long for the church and their children and grandchildren to carry it on. I could still see and hear their prayers and songs for us to carry on. I feel bad when I see the churches today. We've let our old people down, no matter what the excuse. The whiteman road is covered or is covering our road.

All the things in today's dominate society (whiteman) are made to take all your attention from which God meant and wants us to have. If our attention isn't on religion, then the dominate society can't get the money he worships. And he'll do any and everything to get it. He is blinded by greed from birth. Religion is in his way, and he goes all out to push it out of your mind. You read and see through the media everyday something has to do with this greed. Kill his own family and plead not guilty. Alcohol, drugs, weapons, you name it, he will use it for his gain. He brought all this, this and more, when he invaded and destroyed our beautiful country and people. He doesn't care about you or God, else he couldn't do these things. The laws he makes don't apply to him. They don't mean anything to him. He'll turn the laws inside out and pound at them so much that after a while they (laws) don't mean a thing. Nitpick them to death. No, he will not accept blame for his own lawbreaking. He will not admit guilt because he will then break the whiteman's code of being pure and innocent. And they can't stand to admit wrong. Have you noticed, in any matter, no matter what, that when this man proposes a policy, law, function, or an agreement that he not take "no" for an answer. It actually shocks him when you say no or anything negative. He can't believe it. He always assumes he'll get what he wants and how you don't want it or to do it. So he makes a law to make you do it. Or else. Every day it just gets worse. One day my dad, back in the fifties, said, "Whiteman is gonna outsmart himself." He already has. The world is a big mess and can't be turned around. As God said, "In this world you will have trouble. But take heart, I have overcome the world." I understand now what He meant. I can live in this world knowing God will see me through it with others who believe. I don't have to be miserable because I understand.

I will give one example of God's power and presence. I wasn't going to write this part in my life, but somehow, someone, somewhere is having trouble may believe and or benefit. I spoke of AA meetings. And the importance of them to people with drinking problems. This is not a blowhard, made up, or taken from somewhere. It's a truly powerful experience. Yes, it happened to me.

I think it was in 1970, and I was in Texas at the time. I was with an Indian woman at the time and had a pretty good job in Mesquite, Texas. There were other Indian families in the immediate [area] that were from towns in Caddo County, Oklahoma. Carnegie, Anadarko, and Apache. On weekends, of course, we'd party, with the drinks. I was doing okay and putting a little money away in a bank. Well, one morning I went out to head to work, only to see an empty parking place. My car was gone. Well, it was stolen, alright, as I had the keys in my pocket. I reported it, and it was put in the Dallas paper, but it was never found. My job was twenty-five miles away, and I had no transportation. I just let that job go and started looking for another. Meantime, this woman and I had been arguing about finding another job. That led to more drinking and arguing.

So one day I came back from job hunting to an empty house; just some of my clothes were left. I checked the bank, and she had cleaned it out, as she had me make a joint account. I guess I wasn't too surprised at that. Having a few clothes, less money, and no car, I eventually had to leave that house for the street. I had friends I'd stay with for a little while but don't like to impose, so I got a small room above a bar I and others drank in, and others close by. I'd head out to this temporary day job to get by until maybe I could get a foothold somewhere. Some days I didn't get sent out on a job. So I just idled the day in a bar. There was a bar where an Indian lady worked days, and we knew each other. She was a Pottawattamie from Kansas. We'd just talk the day, as hardly anybody came into that bar during the day.

I think it was January of 1970. One day, while sitting at the bar talking with this lady's sister, I sorta noticed somebody walk in the door, which was open because Dallas winters aren't too cold. Then somebody tapped me on the shoulder and started laughing. I turned around and see three Indian guys. Two I knew and also knew that their kind have no business in Dallas because people there work, and I know these guys won't work. The third one I didn't know. One was from Carnegie, Oklahoma; the other two were from Cheyenne country in Oklahoma. Sure did surprise me to see them in Dallas. Of all people. How they showed up at that particular bar also got me. But that bar was in East Dallas, by the corner of Peak and Bryan Streets, which every Indian in Dallas knows with all its bars at the time.

Well, we visited for a while before they told me they were going to Albuquerque, New Mexico. Well, I had no business in Albuquerque. I said, hell no, I'm okay right here. They said they were going to just look around and check out the bars for a couple days and come back. I still said no. We got to visiting with those two sisters at the bar, where one worked. One of those guys pushed a beer glass toward me and told me it was vodka. It wasn't quite half a glass full, so I downed it. They were about to leave, so we said our byes. Or thought so.

Now this is bad. I do not remember leaving that bar or Dallas. When I came to, I didn't know where I was but heard a [lot] of laughing. I was with those guys on Interstate 40 somewhere in west Texas. They said I decided to go with them, which I do not believe because that drink they gave me was not vodka but 190 proof Everclear, which looks like vodka but has a mighty kick to it. It's a whiskey, but almost pure alcohol. I was pretty mad at first, but just took some more beer drinking and settled in, thinking they'd bring me back to Dallas like they said. Said they thought I knew Albuquerque and could sorta guide them around. Well, I didn't know anybody in Albuquerque, nor have I ever been there before and know anything about it.

I don't know how they found this bar, but it had a lot of Indians in it. From New Mexico, I assumed. We drank around there 'til closing, then drove out of town, as they had picked up a woman to mess with. I don't know how I ended up driving but guess I and the rest stopped somewhere in the desert outside town. I woke up when my door was yanked open and was looking upside down at a big policeman. We all came to. The policeman asked what we were doing out there. One of the guys said we got lost and ran out of gas. The cop guy gives us some gas and directions to town and to be careful. What?

Anyway, we head back to town to find something to eat. We get some food and go to the University of New Mexico campus and crash out on the campus. That evening or afternoon we head back to that same bar. We were going to leave about nine that night, so don't stray off. We bothered around until this guy tells me we'd be leaving in about fifteen minutes. So I go back to this booth, where I was visiting with some guys for ten more minutes, then left to go back to the guys I was with. Well, I didn't see them and went out to see if they were at their car. The car was gone, so I stood around to see if they changed parking. I walked around the outside of the bar while looking for them. I'd check back in the bar and waited, thinking they'd be looking for me. After about an hour it was beginning to dawn on me that they just left me. Those guys I just met were also looking. Something was telling me what I didn't want to believe. They left me. It was a bad, bad feeling.

In New Mexico, as people out there know, it gets darn cold fast in the evening, and this was January, I think. I was "not" dressed for that kind of cold. I had a tiny jacket that had no lining. No gloves. It was warm in Dallas, but I never thought I'd be in this situation and didn't intend to. I and my acquaintances just hung around the bar, hoping my ride would show up and wanting to believe this really wasn't happening to me. But it was and did happen or planned. As I thought about those guys, I wasn't too surprised they did that. They weren't my usual crowd in Oklahoma. I just knew who they were. Why they did that I don't know, because we got along okay. I was getting desperate as time wore on. I kept watching the clock and the entrance. The guys I was with were from the Laguna Reservation and were just street people. They'd ask me what I was gonna do. I didn't know. Just hoped.

Closing time comes around, and I was getting hopeless and scared. I didn't know anybody in that town or what part I was in. At closing these guys stayed with [me] for a while, but they seemed to just disappear into the night. It was damn cold and getting colder. I walked and tried to find just any kind of shelter. I found this old train depot and got under the dock to find some kind of warmth. That was not going to work. I was going to freeze to death under there, and nobody would know or care. Just another street, homeless winter casualty. Happens all the time to these types. But it was me. I don't belong in this situation.

I tell myself I'd better get up and start walking to try to keep warm anyway. I'm going to freeze to death and knew it. As I walked, I was starting to shake uncontrollably. I wasn't walking; I was shaking and bouncing. I didn't know where, but I was going to just lay down and accept death somewhere. I couldn't see it no other way. About the time of this thought, I seen a small light in what was a fleabag hotel. Before that I actually thought about breaking a store window to go to jail and warmth. But I was too cold to lift anything to do that. So I went into this small hotel and stood by this small heater. I stood at the stove for about five minutes, when the manager told me to get out, as I didn't have a room there. Back on the street and about to lose it, I seen a lighted area just down the street. Seemed a beacon. It was a large Greyhound bus station. There I could warm up a little, if it wasn't just a mirage in my freezing head.

Anyway, it was real, and I go in and sit down, expecting to be told to leave because I didn't have a ticket. After a while the PA system announced that if you didn't have a ticket you'd be asked to leave or police will take you to jail. Right then I didn't care which one happened, but I'd prefer jail. Well, neither one happened, and due to the warmth I soon dozed off, not much caring what happened. I wakened to find somebody punching my leg. It was the Laguna guys I'd met the day before and wondered that I was still around. They suggested we go back to that bar to see if the guys might have showed up to check on me, which I seriously doubted. A pretty thin hope anyway.

We go back to the bar, and nobody's seen them that morning, and I knew they were gone. We hung around looking, anyway. About eleven o'clock that morning a couple of big guys showed up, called my new friends over. They were looking for these guys from the Laguna Rez. They were there to take my friends back to the rez. I got worried again. Now what? Of course, I didn't know why, but I'd be alone again. The now new friends explained to these guys from the rez my situation to them. But it didn't much matter to them; they were taking these guys back.

The friends told me they had to go with these other guys, and what was I gonna do. I told them I was already in a mess here, and I'd just be going farther west. They left it up to me, and, not knowing what else, I just went along with them. What am I getting into? I don't know these people and don't know where I'm going. I don't know what; I just hoped. Laguna Reservation is about seventy miles west of Albuquerque, and I was going deeper into the unknown. All this time I kept hope in prayer and God, although it seemed hopeless at the time.

We arrived in Laguna Pueblo at four o'clock that afternoon and got off at one of the guy's house (adobe). We ate some stew, and he changed clothes, cut some wood, played some basketball. What? How can you relax? Not think about what was happening or going to happen. What kinda people are they? Do my parents know my whereabouts?

After a while they decide to go down the road, where their friend has a bar. We drink a few beers at this bar, I think called "Kings." We wander down the road to another bar. A place called Midway. This little shanty bar off I-40 was to prove the most "awesome" place in my life, as it turns out. Of course, these guys know everybody around there and are known themselves. Introductions are made, and we visit and shoot some pool. The ceiling is bad and broken, but the bar apparently doesn't leak. Real rez bar. It's on a Friday evening, and people start to show up, plus a motley Navajo band from Crownpoint will give some live music. They had what was called a stage and a rather large and beat-up dance floor with old wooden high-backed booths. My friends would bum some wine or beer, as they were apparently broke.

I'm going to put this the best I can. A crowd started to build and of course with some rowdies. We were there about eight o'clock when there was a little disturbance at the bar. Somebody got thrown out into the now snowing night. Of course, it's getting colder, and big snowflakes are really coming down. But a little wind. Turns out the guys that got thrown out were my newfound friends. Can't come back in. Man, oh man. What now? I'm a stranger in a strange place. Surround by Laguna, Acoma, and Navajo people that are mostly young. A door was shut in my face, it seemed. I guess my friends walked off. I have about three dollars left, and I'm cold. The band plays on. Raunchy music, to make matters worse. I don't know why, but I'd go to the door and look out. For what? Are my parents, wife, brother, friend, or girlfriend coming to pick me up? I can't help but watch the clock and wonder when closing time is and what to do then. The snow is getting deeper and deeper. I look up and around the big, bouldered, nearby hills. I'm wondering as I look toward I-40 about a mile and a half away. Walk toward it, climb up into the boulders, and a little windbreak, curl up, and die? I slowly sip my beer and know time is slipping away. About two hours to 2:00 a.m., closing time. What then? I pray some more and take one last look outside before I go back in, say to myself, "Okay, so be it." Well, before I lift my beer up, I feel a gentle tap on my shoulder. I don't know how I looked, but I was looking into a big, cheery face. Not too large but a pleasantly plump woman. She asked what happened to my friends. I told her they got thrown out, and she said, "I know." Guess she had been watching me and knew I wasn't from around there. She asked me about it, and I just told her like it was; she told me to go over to where she and her mom were sitting in a booth. They seemed so concerned and told me so. They kept asking me what I was going to do when it closed. I told them I was going to I-40, but they cut in and said I was going to do no such thing and to just relax my mind and have a beer. They explained who they were (Acoma) and told me I was going with them home. I felt they read my mind! How could this be possible with these people I've not met or seen before. You know what? God knows. Or, why me? Only He knows.

The woman's name is Mae Chavez and her daughter Beverly, who came over to me in that now vacant and empty bar right off Interstate 40 in New Mexico. Acoma or Sky City, New Mexico. They lived in Acomita Pueblo. The old ones and a few others live upon the mesa. Just like they did over one thousand years ago.

I don't have enough praises for these people and God, who worked through them. The next morning upon awakening, I stood at this big window looking toward I-40. And a little traffic going east and west. A little snow was still falling when I heard that same voice I heard last night. "Don't even think about it; come and eat breakfast with us." At breakfast I told them more about me. They told me to just forget about hitchhiking. The storm wasn't going to let up for some time. I assumed they knew what they were talking about. They told me to stay until things warmed up and not to try to test the weather, that I could stay there and maybe find a job around there and save some money if I still wanted to leave. I thought about my situation in Dallas and figured I would find a job and save up. Acoma is about twenty-five miles east of Grants, New Mexico, and very little between. Desert, lava beds, and mountains. They told me to stay away from the uranium mines around there. Said it's too dangerous.

Their adobe house was large enough and had a packed-dirt adobe floor, and you couldn't tell it was made of earth. It was so smooth, hard, and clean. They had two woodstoves. One for front room and the other for the kitchen. Those were the kind of stoves I grew up with in the country, and I liked them. Made me sorta feel like old times. It also was the same old routine. Chop wood, put up kindling, fill the water buckets, and put a kettle on the stove for face washing and dishes. It was so cozy and homelike, and I started to settle in more. I accepted my situation and began to get serious on finding a job.

These people were so down-to-earth and did their best to make me feel at home. Mae Chavez had five daughters and two sons, one was in college at University of New Mexico in Albuquerque. They were, like all the Pueblo tribes were, of the Catholic faith and didn't bug me on my faith. Beverly, the oldest daughter, was two years out of college. Colleen, tenth grade; Della, ninth; Mary, seven grade; and Monica. The youngest son was Gus, third grade. Randy, the oldest. The father of Mae and grandpa to them lived at top of the mesa (Acoma, Sky City). Mae worked as a cook at the Laguna-Acoma School. I did all the chores and liked it. So like home.

Mae gave me the use of her new pickup to job search. There were sawmills scattered around there but not so close by. I was beginning to feel like I may not find a job, as things were far apart. By the time

I contacted Mom, and she about swallowed that phone. What in the world was I doing out there and on and on, but it finally sunk in. But she did send some money for necessities. I could just hear her.

This is kinda weird, but maybe it was supposed to happen that way, and I believe it. I was feeling so down because jobs were few and far apart where I checked. I was about to give up, when I found a sawmill near Milan, which is about a mile west of Grants. I figured I'd hear the same story. Times are slow, not hiring, or when we've got enough, and I did hear it. I talked to the boss there, and he told me the same. Not hiring, etc. I told him my situation and needed a job for at least three or four months and didn't like to impose on people, like where I was staying, even though they didn't mind, as I told them. Make just enough to get me back to where I knew, probably lost what little I had at that room. He wasn't hiring away. So I get up and start to walk off. Then he hollers at me and says, "Wait, I'm going to go ahead and hire you, as I like your looks." What? Oh no, I don't want the job. But he said, "Oh, I'm sorry I didn't mean it that way. I was talking about your size compared to these short Indian guys working here, and you said you had experience on the engine lathe and machine-shop machines. Some of the work calls for heavy lifting, and these smaller guys don't lift too much."

So I had a job and told him I need it at least for two or three months. Well, I worked there for about the time I said I would. At the start of my last week there, I reminded him of the deal. That Friday he called me into his office to give me my last check. Only he had changed his mind. He said I was the best worker that ever worked there and was offering me a life-time job. With a darn good raise. He also told me I could work half a day, and he would pay me for a full eight hours with full whatever benefits. All I would be doing was sharpening all those different saw blades from all the machines there with the lathe. Wow! Did this fellow put me on the spot. Years later I would think about that and wish I could kick myself to death for turning him down. I just told him I was sticking to my plan. I had it made and just blew it. A big-time regret in my life.

How could I be so stupid. But I was. I had told Mrs. Chavez of my plan and her family, but I'm sure they didn't believe me and probably thought I was going to marry one of them. They were more family to me than that. Those were beautiful young women, with the Pueblo eyes, skin, and hair. But I tried to be just a big brother to them. They didn't talk to me very much. But I knew something else was going on in their heads. What do you do? They completely trusted me, but I wouldn't have given them reason not to. Access to Mae Chavez's bank, new pickup, and run of the house. I'd go with them to their Pueblo feasts or cultural dances, where I enjoyed their dancing and singing. Sat on the mesa and watch the beautiful landscapes. And the setting sun. It was good to actually be a part of a family like that. Something in me had changed. I saw things differently. There is a God, and He's real. I know, I saw Him through these people. I can't describe everything that took place there. Just beautiful. I had an experience that I'll never forget. I just wish at times that I could redo all that out there. Sadly, I was not of sound mind when I decided to leave Acoma Pueblo. I had everything I needed with the Chavez family. I think about them many times and wonder at it all. Was it real? Yes.

One day at work I had an accident, which I could have avoided, as I knew better. I fractured my right wrist, and the doctor set my wrist and braced it. You know, those girls would argue over who was going to wash my face, shave me, or trim and comb my hair. Lol! I was treated like a king.

Well, the worse thing that could happen to them did. I got home from work, and Beverly drove me to a cleaners in Grants to pick up some clothes. When we got back to the house, I did not want to do this, but I did. I announced to the girls that I was leaving as planned. That house so quiet it was eerie. Della went to the couch and flopped down on her stomach and just bawled. God, that got me! Beautiful Colleen got so quiet and turned away crying I did not want to see that. I hurt these girls so bad, and I felt so low-life and guilty and so mixed up. What have I done to this beautiful family.

I felt so bad and sick. Della just said she wished she had never met me. I don't [know] if I've ever felt so low. I let them down but never knew it was that much. I didn't know I meant so much to them. I figured I'd better go on; I think I ruined something here. It's gonna follow me. I guess I left my heart in Acomita Pueblo.

I met several people in the Pueblos, and they surprised me by giving a little going-away party, which made me feel worse. Then on to catch a bus in Grants to Dallas. I had a pint of vodka, but one woman gave me another one, with a turquoise ring. All this time I'm so mixed up, jump off the bus or go on as it was pulling out of the depot. I glanced out and saw something I never expected. Seemed like half the Pueblo was there running beside the bus and yelling for me not to go. What a way to go or see. I just stayed "buzzed up" all the way to Dallas. Of course, I found nothing of mine in Dallas. Just a big, empty feeling.

A few years after that, I made several trips to New Mexico to Gallup ceremonies or just looked around. Taos, Zuni, and others. Most every time I went, I stopped by Acoma and look around. Hurts though. I always carry these people in my heart, wishing at what might have been. I found Mae Chavez on two of my trips out there, then one of her daughters who didn't quite remember me at first. Once I gave Mae Chavez a hundred-dollar bill but felt so stupid later. I could never pay them what I feel I owe them. When I'm leaving New Mexico, I feel so bad as I watch the mountains fade away. I want to go back. It can never be the same.

One time Pat Hollingshead [and I] were on I-40 going west and seen the exit to Laguna Pueblo. I turned off to see if I could find that bar I was talking about earlier. And, my gosh, I found it. I was so overwhelmed, it hurt. Just think, I was in that bar one cold and snowy night. One desperate, scared individual giving up on my life. Thirty years ago, a lonesome, desolate, vacant building now with a few tattered banners flying in the ghostly wind, I cannot describe the feeling. Hard to believe what happened in that building. We just sat there for a while, as I bowed my head to God. She just had to ask me, "What are we doing here? Are you okay?" I just said, "This is where I met the angels." That statement is so true, so help me God. Of course, she would never know or understand what took place in that very building. It's like a shrine to me, and few, if any, would understand.

In my most desperate and darkest hour, God came to me through his angels, Mae and Beverly Chavez. A true miracle came to me that night. I will always speak of my God and what He did for me. "I will never leave you or forsake you." Miracles happen every day. But we won't acknowledge them. He woke you up this morning, didn't He? At what few times I've told this, like in a testimony or AA meeting, I'm sometimes asked to retell it. I don't mind. I hope somebody will believe and accept the truth. And that's just one of many times when God walked with me, and I don't realize it. What does it take?

I told the guys back home that I herded sheep around that mesa. They had a flock of sheep that Mae Chavez's father would take out every day to feed. One day he wasn't feeling up to the task, so Mae asked me if I would [do] it. Once I would I said. She explained a few things to me, so it seemed easy enough. They also had a sheepdog, which knew exactly what to do anyway. Back home I told them, "I was watching over my flock by night. With my staff." Right away, Spi said, "You mean you were like the shepherds in the Christmas story?" Lol! But there I was with my flock. I even thought about what Spi said while I out there doing that. I thought, boy, if they could see me now; how do I get into these kinda situations?

Never in my life would I even dream something like that would happen to me. Yes sir, God took me and showed me something that certainly changed something in me, and I never thought I would tell that story to anyone. In God's book the passage says, "And do not forget to entertain strangers, for you may be entertaining angels." And not know it. Ay-o-b'awy-daw, it's the truth.

Some days, while alone at my camp by the creek at our old place in the country, I'd sit and reminisce about these things. Some are hard to believe, yet they did happen to me. I been a long way, and here I am back home. It's all gone here now. How could it be that all the people, all the so many things that took place, are gone. I walk where our old trails were and remember what took place right where I'm standing. Where are they? Why just me left? The wind, the little water sounds, the little birds, the rustle of the dry leaves, they tell me. It's supposed to be that way. But what happened to the little boy who used to play, fish, swim, and dream here? They tell me that too, and I find peace here. The little birds see me and talk about what their great grandpa's stories told about me. So they know who I am.

I've been through two broken marriages, so two divorces. Many jobs, good and bad. An administrative specialist in the U.S. Air Force. Played many baseball and fast-pitch softball [games] as a pitcher. I lost two sons. My third son, who I named Clifton Ray, and Raymond Lee. Clifton Ray was all of six months in this world. Raymond Lee was Ponca and Kiowa. Passed away at thirty-two, going on thirty-three. Clifton Ray had a Kiowa mother. My oldest son, Byron Scott, Kiowa, is fifty-one, I think. Zame-t'ay! Sometimes I lose count. Byron has a brother, a brother whose mom is Ponca. Rae Denise Tongkeamha Buck is my oldest daughter and is Kiowa, Byron's sister, who is the oldest of my children. Denise has a sister, Stephanie Tongkeamha Garcia, a member of the Seminole Tribe of Florida. All my kids are and were athletes, and I'm so proud of all of them and love them so much. They are God's gifts to me. And God does not make mistakes. I've wished I could have done more for them and still wish that. I want all of them to come to and know and accept Jesus Christ as their lord and savior. In fact, I wish all my family would; if you look long, hard, and sincerely, you will find Him.

Within a five to six year period, I lost a large part of my family. Wallace, Clifton, Dad and Lavena, and James. Brothers and sisters and my father. I was down to my mom when I moved back from Dallas, Texas, to stay and help Mom. Well, she also passed on. What to do now? I'm so lost. It seemed like I was hit from all sides already. Then my close sister, Melissa, passes away. What does this mean for me? I'm down to my two youngest sisters, Prenella and Lisa. I have to carry on and be strong for them.

The logical choice was to just pick up the tools that were laid at my feet by Dad and Mom through God. His word is my toolbox to fix things and carry on. That's why I'm so glad I have deep Christian roots through my elders and family. I get even stronger and more understanding than I ever did as I know more and more about what God wants me to know. When I lost Mom, I felt like I was stuck in one place now. There isn't any kind of the work that I do in Carnegie. No machine shops or large printing companies. I just did odd jobs here and there until I heard about this vocational technology school in nearby Fort Cobb. I enrolled and took several different classes to be doing something. The classes I took were automotive (brakes and bearings specialist). Unarmed and armed security guard, and even thought I was a printer. I took another print class. Lol, I even got my GED done there. I had finished my eleventh year in high school, left, got married, and volunteered into the U.S. Air Force. This elder woman teacher there talked me into doing the GED thing. Rats, it was so simple. Don't know why it took me so long to do that. Then this woman talks me into some college courses. Think I took four or five of these electives through Redlands Community College in El Reno, Oklahoma, and USAO in Chickasha, Oklahoma.

Well, I needed a job and money, so I started looking for work. I seen a Kiowa Tribe ad wanting someone to drive a Kiowa Fas-Trans bus. I never really did like to drive, but I was getting desperate. For a job and money. So I go and apply, kinda half-heartedly. I got hired but was told I needed a CDL license. I just had the regular driver's license. So back to that vo-tech for truck-driving school. I passed all seven tests with ease and passenger and hazmat endorsements. I had a route to Anadarko, Apache, Lawton, and back to Carnegie. That job lasted about ten months and was shut down.

As young teens, we hitchhiked a lot. It didn't seem too out of place then, and you didn't have too much trouble getting a ride. We thought [it] was fun and an adventure. To be on your own and sorta free. We were told of the dangers that may come, but we didn't give it too much thought. We hitchhiked to "bop-hops" or powwows around the towns in the area. We figured we'd catch a ride back with someone from our area. Lol. And sometimes we didn't catch a ride back. Stranded, we just crashed wherever and hit the road the next day. I was sometimes more fortunate than my friends. The powwows were usually three days, and if I didn't make it home sometime, I didn't worry too much because I knew the folks would be back the next day with some clean clothes and food for me. Me, aw-dae? My p'ah-bees would say, "Damn that guy." Mom did not like to see me dirty.

There's a certain stage when teenagers that I'm sure we all went through. I'm guilty of that. A sort of rebellion at authority. Some have it more or less than others. Your mind and body goes through this change, and you don't rightly know how to handle it. So you argue with your sibs and parents. You'll see it in your own kids. And you actually think you're right. Sadly, some seem to have a hard time ever growing out of it. It all starts in the home, and if the home is stable, you should have a good handle on life. Having God in a home is a home indeed. I remember Dad would say, "If you don't have love, compassion, and God in your home, then that's not a home, it's just a building."

We had a beautiful home in the country with a beautiful setting. We had all we needed that money couldn't buy. So many relatives just down the road, and so many things to do. We had time to be family. If times were hard, we didn't seem to think so. It was natural to us, and we just went on about it. I didn't give too much thought to change. Even though I didn't give it permission, change entered my life.

I must have been about fourteen years old when I first got drunk. I got with a bunch in town that were about one or two years older than me. It was also my birthday, so they wanted me to celebrate it. We drove to Anadarko after seeing a bootlegger in Carnegie. I didn't even know what a bootlegger was. They got what they called a fifth of wine. We just drove around, and they knew of another bootlegger in Anadarko. They were laughing and seem to be enjoying themselves. I just acted like I knew what it was all about. On the way back to Carnegie, they told me to celebrate my birthday by taking a drink with them. This girl told me not to several times. Then I thought, what the heck, may as well, because they kinda made sense to me at that time. You know it tasted good, and I didn't think it was just some kind a sweet drink. We drove around some more, and sometime later I started feeling pretty good and laughed at everything. I didn't know what was happening to me, while they knew and were cracking up to see me like that. I didn't feel or see anything wrong with that. Later on they figured they better take me home, but I didn't want to, so I got off at my aunt Adelaide Little Chief's house. When I got off the car, I stood up and fell flat on my face. The ground wouldn't stop moving. Anyway, I think I scared the hell outta my aunt. Course I wouldn't do it again. But I did, and again and again.

I can't undo my experience in that alcoholic world, but I can tell you all about it. It (alcohol) has no respect for people from all walks of life. It's best not to even try to test its power. Especially those who have or think they have flaws in life. Alcohol will not make things better. It'll do just the opposite. It seems innocent enough by many to try it. The devil works in that bottle, fueled by man's greed for money. He doesn't care about you or that it will kill you; he makes money off your misery and death. From it, I've seen doctors, judges, lawyers, police, highlifes, and lowlifes with the same disease, and it is a disease all suffer from it. I've been sober for twenty-five years so far and will stay sober forever. God did for me what was not humanly possible. Remember, we do nothing good for ourselves; God does that. So if you had a problem with alcohol and are now sober, you didn't do it all by yourselves. God gets the credit for all good things. I still go to AA meetings even after twenty-five years of sobriety. It's something I do, though some people would wonder why. It's just like going to church. It's a part of me, and it's never boring. I get something out of it each time I go. I do not look down on people who drink or liquor itself. I have nothing to do with it. It's just like I never took a drink before. God can do for us what we cannot do for ourselves. With God, all things are possible. Yes, even for you. I walked in darkness one time, but God also walked with me. I am one of God's miracles and will never forget.

I believe I walked around this big circle so as to experience what I wondered about. God never left me. He showed me the other kind of life and led me back to Him. I was severely punished for wanting that kind of life. I won't go into it, but I, according to the doctors, lost my earthly life twice during those times. Of course, I didn't know that until later, when these doctors told me. These occurred in different years. It's not by luck or being fortunate that I'm still here. It's by God's grace. He has yet work for me to do. All His words in His book, the Bible, are so true. You can go to church twelve days of the week, but if you doubt God's word, you go for nothing. Praying or just walking into a church isn't going to change or save you. You have to live God's word every moment and work it. If you aren't honest or sincere in prayer or church, God will know it. And you wonder why your prayers aren't answered. He created you and therefore knows all about you.

God answers prayers, but sometimes we wonder if He does. His answers come, just not the way we expected them. Or when we expect them. We just trust Him. If you're sincere, your prayer is heard. Don't wait or look for them to be answered. He knows. Remember, you cannot worship God and money. Today's technology is blocking out God's word. People are actually believing they can have a better life and live longer by science. Technology can never do what God can. And you can't or don't buy that. It's free. If you think you can be a member of two kinds of churches and still serve God, forget it. It's never worked and never will.

God is not concerned about how you look or what you wear to church. He looks at the heart to see if He's there. People will dress "to the nines," sing along, listen to a forever sermon, and pray for one hour. When they leave the church, they feel good and smile around. They feel good and find relief from a false worship. They are just relieved to be outta there. Now they can go back to being their real selves. When you leave the church, take it with you. I could go on and on about God, but most people don't want to hear that. They want to know what makes you tick.

In 2001 I was job searching around Lawton, which is fifty miles south of Carnegie. I was about to give it up, when on the way to Carnegie I was passing by the Comanche Complex because I seen three new busses parked there. I heard they were starting a transit system like the Kiowa Fas-Trans. I wasn't too interested in that, but I thought, what the heck. At the Comanche Complex I filled out the application. Upon talking to the interviewer, I found out she was my sister from the Giemausaddle Kiowa family side and half-Comanche. They told me I was just the sort they were looking for and hired me. I had all I needed for the job. I thought I would do the job for a year and move to Montana to stay with my Crow family. Anyway, after about eight months I was kept pretty busy and was getting to even like that kind of driving. So I stayed on for a little over ten years. Even made a couple of special trips to Idaho and the other nearby states up there. I took the Comanche Little Ponies up there to the Fort Hall Shoshone-Bannock Festival or powwow. That was the biggest and best powwow I had seen so far and sure did like it. I am a member of the Comanche Ponies but didn't dance the first trip. I liked it so much that, on my next two two-week vacations, I drove back up there, only without my crew and bus. So I made four trips up there to see the powwow. For one thing, they had forty drums there and contested into the wee hours. That was in August, but it got pretty cold at night. It didn't seem to bother them. I thought, these were real powwowers.

In early 2011 I was diagnosed with the dreaded "C" word, cancer. In April of that year, I started radiation and chemotherapy for six months. I was kept on the Comanche payroll all that time, as they wanted me back to work after the treatment. At first I did not want to go through the treatment. I did not think that would ever happen to me but it did, and I hated the radiation and chemo. I mean, it took everything out of me, and [I] was not expected to make it. I have never been so sick. I even told myself I was sick. I talked to God and accepted His word, "Everything I do for you is for the good." I told my family that however things come out through this, death or cure, is still God's will for me, and I know God does not lie or make mistakes. Although taken to the very edge and end of my rope, God did not leave me. He saw me through. I did not give up or quit, even though I don't remember most of it. I was in the hospital for thirty-one days after five days of chemo. That was because I was given a larger dose of chemo, so they could knock it down, so they could treat it sooner or easier. They didn't tell me that until later, when I went back for a checkup. Talk about being mad. I thought, "It's a good thing I was so weak at the time." I had lost forty-five pounds and can't gain it back, plus all the side effects, which are with me today. Anybody that has gone through that will know what I'm talking about.

I went back and drove for about a week, and I knew I was not able to anymore, so resigned and retired from the workforce. I was about five years past full retirement age anyway and was getting my regular work wages and Social Security checks anyway. Just had to "throw my towel in." And anybody who's on Social Security is not rich and have to adjust. At times I'd wish I was still working. I still am up at 3:00 a.m. and try to stay busy somehow. I have two hearing aids, full dentures, constant pain, wear glasses, and my medicines. Lol! And to think, "Once upon a time." I look around some days and think, "Where are all my p'ah-bees (brothers, etc.) gone?" All that were my age and a little younger have all gone home. Nobody to talk with or reminisce with. Can't say, "Remember so and so?" Or what we did then, and how we used to do things. It gets boring and hard at times, but when I read God's work in daily devotionals, I know that's exactly the way it's supposed to be, according to His plans for me. He still walks with me. "23rd Psalm."

One of the people I met on my journey is a person I came to know as my nephew, who is an adopted son of my brother Clifton, who has gone on home. Benjamin (Ben) Kracht is my nephew or son now. He is a native of Indiana, an anthropologist, professor of Native studies, author. He teaches at Northeastern State University in Tahlequah, Oklahoma. Pardon me if I got his title wrong. If I wish I could do it all over again, then I should perish the thought. My nephew, who I described, is a big part of my life now. He comes to visit me, and I always enjoy his time with me. He loves these mountains here, like I do. Ben also has a son, Robbie [Rob], whom I think of just as much, for he's my "k'ohn" [grandson]. I know they will always be Kiowas at heart and a part of the Tongkeamha [family] and legacy. I thank God for them being with us.

My kids, grandkids, and great-grandkids are scattered from Oklahoma to Texas, Kansas, Florida, Arizona, South Dakota, Montana, and probably others I'm not aware of. And yes, they're part Kiowa and other tribes. I'm always thinking of them and pray that I would see them one day. Yet I know that's farfetched because, like others at my age, my days are numbered. I know that, and I know everything won't get done.

Every day is a new opportunity to get something done until I'm called. I still go hunting and fishing or camping at my creek. That's good enough for me. It's good to enjoy life because that's what God wants for us. That's what I want my kids to do. Enjoy the life God gave us. I hope they all let Him into their life. I want them to know God. It's okay to lean on Him. When we fear, or doubt, or don't trust Him, we turn our backs to Him, and He'll do the same to you. "I will come and remove your lamp from its stand."

I know I didn't say it all in this writing, but it would be too much and too long. I put down what mostly comes to mind. I didn't even intend to go this far, but I just felt like I'll leave a little something about me. I know we all go pretty deep. I was blessed to have seen, done, or experienced the old Kiowa ways since 1942 to today. I have seen the changes, and it saddens me. Where are the Kiowa? I believe I'm going to see all the old people I came from, and all will be like the old days, when there were just us Natives here.

# NOTES

Face-to-face interviews with Henrietta Tongkeamha in 1993 are cited as "H. Tongkeamha, interview." Face-to-face data obtained during ethnographic field trips to Kiowa country in 1993 and between 2017 and 2019 are cited as "Kracht, field notes." During the writing and revision stages of this project— July 2018 through February 2021—Raymond and I communicated through phone texts, a useful method for obtaining quick answers to my questions, especially during the COVID-19 pandemic, which prevented me from traveling to Lawton. Throughout the project Lisa and I communicated using Facebook messenger. All her quotes and passages were submitted using this platform.

## INTRODUCTION

1. The Tongkeamha homestead is approximately eight miles northeast of the church. Raymond Tongkeamha, text message to Benjamin Kracht, May 23, 2020.
2. Meers Store and Restaurant, the extant building from a gold rush town established in 1901, is located in the foothills of the Wichita Mountains on the Meers Fault at the intersection of State Highway 115 and NW Meers Porter Hill Road. The restaurant is renowned for its longhorn Meersburgers.
3. "Wichita Mountains."
4. Collectively, the tribes are referred to as the KCA Indians.
5. The other communities included (1) Mount Scott/Meers, immediately north of Fort Sill; (2) Sugar Creek, ten miles west of Saddle Mountain; (3) Cedar Creek, east of modern Carnegie; (4) Stinking Creek, south of Carnegie; (5) Samone, west of Carnegie; (6) Elk Creek, near present-day Hobart and Lone Wolf; (7) Rainy Mountain Creek, southwest of modern Mountain View; (8) Hog Creek, several miles west of the Anadarko Agency; and (9) Red Stone, several miles west of Hog Creek. Some graduates of Carlisle Indian Industrial School lived near the agency in Anadarko.
6. R. Tongkeamha, text message to Kracht, May 23, 2020.

7. According to Raymond, Apayyat and Oyebi are the same name. They roughly mean "hard to catch" or "to move around," perhaps referring to playing a game. Kracht, field notes, May 30, 2018.

8. Henrietta and Weiser Tongkeamha, taped interview with Kracht, April 14, 1987.

9. Weiser died on March 14, 1991. W. Tongkeamha, taped interview with Kracht, February 3, 1991; Henrietta Tongkeamha, taped interviews with Kracht, May 28, June 2, 4, 1993. Henrietta passed away on November 7, 1993.

10. In 2018 the dance was moved to tribal property south of the Kiowa Tribal Complex.

11. Gretchen Bataille and Kathleen Sands (1994, 188) observe that men's autobiographies highlight public lives, whereas women's "focus on private lives—the examination of personal relationships and individual growth, concentrating on everyday events and activities." In this regard Henrietta's memoirs are similar to *Red Mother: The Life Story of Pretty-Shield, Medicine-woman of the Crows* (Linderman 1932).

12. Lisa Tongkeamha LaBrada, Facebook direct message to Kracht, February 3, 2020.

13. Tongkeamha LaBrada, Facebook direct message to Kracht, July 23, 2018.

14. Tongkeamha LaBrada, Facebook direct message to Kracht, July 23, 2018. Red Buffalo Hall is part of the Kiowa Tribal Complex on the western outskirts of Carnegie, Oklahoma.

15. Tongkeamha LaBrada, Facebook direct message to Kracht, July 25, 2018.

16. Kracht, field notes, September 29, 2017. NDN soup is made with dried corn and beef stew meat. I traveled to Alden with a sad heart, as my father had passed away the previous day, but I knew he supported this venture and was with me in spirit. Two days later I drove to my hometown in northwest Indiana for his funeral.

17. Copies are archived at the American Philosophical Society in Philadelphia.

18. Kracht, field journal, May 18–June 1, 2018; June 30–July 2, November 8–10, December 27–29, 2019.

## 1. HENRIETTA TONGKEAMHA'S MEMOIRS

1. Raymond Tongkeamha, text message to Benjamin Kracht, May 26, 2020.

2. R. Tongkeamha to Kracht, field notes, May 29, 2018.

3. Kiowa County Historical Society, "Town of Gotebo."

4. "Mapping."

5. A contemporary, Charley Apekaum (Charcoal), lived in the Mount Scott/ Meers community and was an active member of the Native American Church. His autobiography, narrated to Weston LaBarre during the summer of 1936, provides lots of information about the Peyote religion in the early twentieth century (see LaBarre 1957).

6. Isabel Crawford funeral program, Dodd Funeral Home, Saddle Mountain Indian Mission, November 22, 1961.

7. Henrietta Tongkeamha, interview with Kracht, May 24, 1993.

8. R. Tongkeamha, text message to Kracht, July 14, 2018.

9. H. Tongkeamha, interview with Kracht, June 4, 1993.

10. H. Tongkeamha, interview with Kracht, June 4, 1993.

11. H. Tongkeamha, interview with Kracht, June 4, 1993.

12. H. Tongkeamha, interview with Kracht, June 4, 1993.

13. R. Tongkeamha, text message to Kracht, September 27, 2019.

14. Shelley Tongkeamha, conversation with Kracht, July 4, 2018.

15. Kracht, field notes, May 17, 21, 1993; H. Tongkeamha, taped interviews with Kracht, May 24, June 2, 4, 1993.

16. Sometime in the early 1990s, the Sand Creek Massacre Descendants Trust, led by Homer Flute, Thompson Flute Jr., Robert Simpson, and Dorothy Wood, filed a petition seeking reparations for the mismanagement of tribal trust funds and atrocities committed on their ancestors in southeastern Colorado by the U.S. Army on November 29, 1864. While conducting fieldwork in May 1993, I recall Dorothy and Homer diligently working on the suit, which was dismissed in October 2016 by the U.S. Supreme Court. The court ruled in *Flute v. United States* (137 U.S. 146 [2016]) that reparations were barred by the doctrine of sovereign immunity. In the interim many hopeful Kiowas researched family trees for Cheyenne descent. Henrietta's first "Indian name" attests to her heritage. Grandparents sometimes bestow Indian names on ɔde, "special," grandchildren by grandparents. Everyone doesn't have an Indian name.

17. In Oklahoma parlance dinner is the noon meal and supper is the evening meal.

18. Tom was drafted into the U.S. Army on September 5, 1918. After reporting to Camp Logan, Texas, on October 18, he was transferred to Company C of the Eightieth Infantry. Tom's military service was brief, for he was honorably discharged on January 30, 1919. "Indians in World War I," BIA General Records 610, Fort Worth Federal Archives Center, Fort Worth, Texas.

19. Years ago Lisa and her mother were driving west on State Highway 153 to Colony so Henrietta could visit a Cheyenne lady and get some sinew from Dora Saumpty. Near the town of Cordell, Henrietta had Lisa stop the car so she could pick some honeysuckles growing in the ditch. Lisa was impressed how her mom slowly crawled into the ditch to get to them. Once Raymond and I were walking around the old dance grounds at Dietrich's Lake, and he picked some flowers and put them on his fingertips in remembrance of his mother's story. Lisa Tongkeamha LaBrada, Facebook direct message to Kracht, July 23, 2018; Kracht, field notes, June 30, 2019.

20. It's possible that among the "Apache tribe" she didn't know was Joe Blackbear (a.k.a. Jim Whitewolf), a Plains Apache Peyotist whose autobiography was published by Charles S. Brant (1969).

21. Many parents feared sending their children to school after a January 1891 incident, in which two boys whipped by a teacher fled the Anadarko Boarding School and froze to death in a blizzard (see Mooney 1898, 360–61, 376).

22. H. Tongkeamha, interview with Kracht, June 4, 1993.

23. From "I remember when": H. Tongkeamha, interview with Kracht, June 4, 1993.

24. H. Tongkeamha, interview with Kracht, June 4, 1993.

25. Atwater Onco (alt. Anko, 1923–2005) was a descendant of calendar keepers and kept a ledger book of tribal genealogy and history. (In May 1993 Atwater led a group of seniors to Cutthroat Gap, site of the Kiowa encampment attacked by an Osage war party in 1833. Holding his gigantic ledger book, Atwater read the names of the Kiowas killed in the massacre.)

26. H. Tongkeamha, interview with Kracht, June 4, 1993.

27. H. Tongkeamha, interview with Kracht, June 4, 1993.

28. H. Tongkeamha, interview with Kracht, June 4, 1993.

29. H. Tongkeamha, interview with Kracht, June 4, 1993.

30. H. Tongkeamha, interview with Kracht, June 4, 1993.

31. From "That was my second time": H. Tongkeamha, interview with Kracht, June 4, 1993.

32. Located north of Ponca City, Chilocco Indian School operated from 1884 to 1980. From "I heard she went": H. Tongkeamha, interview with Kracht, June 4, 1993.

33. From "They want us all": H. Tongkeamha, interview with Kracht, June 4, 1993.

34. From "They'd snitch on you": H. Tongkeamha, interview with Kracht, June 4, 1993.

35. H. Tongkeamha, interview with Kracht, June 4, 1993.
36. From "And then the girls": H. Tongkeamha, interview with Kracht, June 4, 1993.
37. H. Tongkeamha, interview with Kracht, June 4, 1993.
38. From "I made the basketball team": H. Tongkeamha, interview with Kracht, June 4, 1993.
39. James Auchiah (1906–74) was one of the noted Kiowa Six. In the late 1920s Auchiah joined Jack Hokeah, Monroe Tsatoke, Spencer Asah, Stephen Mopope, and Lois Smokey at the University of Oklahoma, where they developed the two-dimensional painting style known as the Kiowa, or Southern Plains School (Wycoff 2004).
40. In indigenous times stories were told at night during the winter (Bierhorst 1985, 6–7).
41. See Ewers (1978).
42. Lucius Aitson, "Killed Him on the Sly" (1865–1918), was the son of Mokeen and Akeen-tay. The first Kiowa pastor at Saddle Mountain Church, he died in 1918 during the influenza pandemic (Kracht 2017, 162, 267; Crawford 1915, 33–34; Corwin 1959, 80–81).
43. Isabel Crawford's funeral was November 22, 1961.
44. One day when Lisa and her mom were passing by the abandoned Kolan-on-da-mah/Odlepaugh allotment, they drove onto the property to look around. Henrietta found an old shoe that she kept as a memento. Tongkeamha LaBrada, Facebook direct message to Kracht, July 30, 2018.
45. H. Tongkeamha, interview with Kracht, May 24, 1993.
46. H. Tongkeamha, interview with Kracht, May 24, 1993.
47. H. Tongkeamha, interview with Kracht, May 24, 1993.
48. H. Tongkeamha, interview with Kracht, May 24, 1993.
49. Born and raised in northern Mexico, Mo-keen (ca. 1849–1934) was about ten years old when he encountered a Kiowa war party and voluntarily joined the tribe. Taken in by Onsokyapta, "Long Foot," keeper of Taime, the Sun Dance bundle, Mo-keen eventually became his assistant and inherited a Taime image. Accordingly, Mo-keen married Akeen-tay, Odlepaugh's mother, following the death of Set'aide, her husband (she was one of four wives). Mo-keen became Odlepaugh's stepfather. Mo-keen and Akeen-tay's son was Lucius Aitson. Mo-keen converted to Christianity following Lucius's death (Kracht 2017, 162, 267; Crawford 1915, 33–34; Corwin 1959, 80–81). (Lucius's birthdate [1865] is not logical because Set'aide lived until 1878.)

50. Note that Billy High Methvin (Apache) was not descended from Rev. J. J. Methvin (Methodist), who began mission work among the Kiowas in the fall of 1887 (see Kracht 2018, 40–49). Raymond notes that "sometimes people got named for someone they considered important, or the government gave them a name"—for instance, Dr. Weiser (Weiser Tongkeamha) and Gen. Ranald S. Mackenzie (Parker McKenzie). Always the teaser, Weiser jokingly called him "Billy High Tailed It," or "Billy Hang Um High." R. Tongkeamha, text message to Kracht, July 6, 2020.

51. There were two hospitals for tubercular patients in Talihina: the Choctaw-Chickasaw Indian Hospital, which opened in 1916, and Eastern Oklahoma Tuberculosis Sanatorium, which began receiving patients in 1921.

## 2. RAYMOND TONGKEAMHA'S MEMOIRS

1. Kiowa kinship is a generational kin, or Hawaiian, type of kinship system. Relatives are classified by gender and generation. With exceptions collateral kin in the grandparents' generation are called grandparents, those in the parents' generation are parents, relatives in the person of reference's generation are siblings, and so on (Kracht 2017, 39–40).

2. Raymond Tongkeamha, text message to Benjamin Kracht, September 30, 2019; Kracht, field notes, May 22, 25, 2018.

3. Chester Horse (b. 1931) is a renowned artist. On February 2, 2020, I met him at Cache Creek United Methodist Church, where a homecoming celebration was held for his eighty-ninth birthday.

4. At '49 dances, songs known as '49s are performed. See chapter 2, note 16.

5. Kiowa elders tell stories about their grandparents standing outside storm shelters, arms raised toward oncoming storms to send away tornados (Kracht 2017, 65–66; 2018, 252). Odlepaugh died seven years earlier.

6. Kiowas fear owls as harbingers of death believed to be the spirits of recently deceased people. Encountering an owl is a frightful experience (Kracht 2017, 68–71; 2018, 247–48).

7. The Battle of Chosin Reservoir, or Chosin Reservoir Campaign, was fought on rough terrain in northeastern North Korea during bitterly cold weather, November 26 to December 13, 1950.

8. Alice B. Kehoe (pers. comm., June 16, 2020) suggests that "Kiowa" derives from the Blackfeet word for "bear," *kyaio*. Bears are often seen on the mountainside above the town. Notably, Kiowas are brothers and sisters to the bear. This close kinship is recognizable through the names of

nineteenth-century men: Stumbling Bear, Afraid-of-Bears, White Bear, Sitting Bear, Mountain Bear, Sky Bear, and so on.

9. No longer visible at the juncture of State Highways 58 and 19 is the Peaville Corner Store. An all-Indian team, the Peaville Sluggers, played on the nearby baseball diamond. Oral traditions abound about the famous "Peaville Rally," when the Sluggers rallied to overcome a double-digit deficit in late innings. Years later several Kiowas attending a baseball game in Saint Louis heard someone in the crowd holler, "Peaville Rally!" as the Cardinals came from behind to beat the visiting team. Several people—including Weiser—told Raymond this story, but he thinks it originated from Clifton, who worked in Saint Louis in the early 1960s. R. Tongkeamha, interview with Kracht, June 30, 2019.

10. The check was probably from the leaseman who farmed her allotment. R. Tongkeamha, text message to Kracht, June 2, 2020.

11. For several decades after World War II, pilots flew over rural western Oklahoma and the Texas Panhandle delivering the Sunday edition of the *Oklahoman*. Marks painted on roofs signified route customers (Lee 1993).

12. Inspired by the story of Kiowa Jim trekking cross-country to church, Raymond and Roderick "Smokey" Gwoompi once decided to hike the same route. The hills, covered by a medley of limestone boulders, stunted trees, brush, and grass, presented a challenging climb. As they crested a hill, another one appeared, then another, so it took them six or seven hours to reach the church, where they had been tasked with cleaning family gravesites before Memorial Day. R. Tongkeamha, text message to Kracht, September 30, 2019.

13. On Saturday, February 1, 2020, I drove from Tulsa to Apache to meet Raymond and was surprised that he was already home from a funeral. He told me he left early when some mourners began singing Peyote songs in the church. Although many Kiowas are tolerant of the Native American Church, some, like Raymond, still oppose peyote and believe it's a drug (see Kracht 2018, 189–90).

14. Kiowa folklore includes stories about chthonic beings and the humans who receive power from them, like Tonakɔt, "Snapping Turtle," a great healer and feared sorcerer (see Kracht 2017, 79; 2018, 24, 75, 79–81, 84, 119).

15. This expression was used as pejorative slang for the oiled hair of African Americans.

16. Associated with powwows, '49s gained popularity in western Oklahoma after 1920, with the success of the Craterville and Anadarko Indian fairs. Held late at night away from powwow grounds, '49s are flirtatious social dances oftentimes accompanied by alcohol consumption. In July 1985 and 1986, Clifton took me to "Greg's Corner," southeast of Carnegie, for '49s during the Gourd Clan ceremonials.

# REFERENCES

Allen, James, Hilton Als, John Lewis, and Leon F. Litwack. 2000. *Without Sanctuary: Lynching Photography in America*. Santa Fe NM: Twin Palms.

Bataille, Gretchen M., and Kathleen M. Sands. 1994. "Women's Autobiography." In *Dictionary of Native American Literature*, edited by Andrew Wiget, 187–92. New York: Garland.

Bell, Betty, Marilyn Buzbee, and Carolyn Riffel, eds. 2001. *Anadarko: "Our First 100 Years," 1901–2001*. Oklahoma City: Globe Color.

Bierhorst, John. 1985. *The Mythology of North America*. New York: Morrow.

Brant, Charles S., ed. 1969. *Jim Whitewolf: The Life of a Kiowa Apache Indian*. New York: Dover.

Corwin, Hugh D. 1959. *Comanche and Kiowa Captives in Oklahoma and Texas*. Guthrie OK: Cooperative.

Crawford, Isabel. [1909?]. *From Tent to Chapel at Saddle Mountain*. Edited by Mary G. Burdette. Chicago: Woman's Baptist Home Mission Society.

———. 1915. *Kiowa: The History of a Blanket Indian Mission*. New York: Revell.

———. 1951. *Joyful Journey: Highlights on the High Way*. Philadelphia: Judson.

Doyah, Ray C. 2003. *Powwow Chairs*. Anadarko OK: Zo'dle-toh.

Ellis, Clyde. 1996. *To Change Them Forever: Indian Education at the Rainy Mountain Boarding School, 1893–1920*. Norman: University of Oklahoma Press.

Ewers, John C. 1978. *Murals in the Round: Painted Tipis of the Kiowa and Kiowa-Apache Indians*. Washington DC: Smithsonian Institution Press.

Greene, Candace S. 2009. *One Hundred Summers: A Calendar Record*. Lincoln: University of Nebraska Press.

Haas, Lisbeth. 2011. *Pablo Tac, Indigenous Scholar*. Berkeley: University of California Press.

Hall, Harlan (Tōćákút). 2000. *Remember, We Are Kiowas: 101 Kiowa Indian Stories*. Bloomington IN: First Books Library.

Kiowa County Historical Society. "The Town of Gotebo, Oklahoma." Unpublished manuscript, May 29, 2018.

Kracht, Benjamin R. 2012. "'It Would Break Our Hearts Not to Have Our Kiowas': War Dancing, Tourism, and the Rise of Powwows in the Early Twentieth Century." *Chronicles of Oklahoma* 90 (3): 286–309.

——. 2017. *Kiowa Belief and Ritual*. Lincoln: University of Nebraska Press.

——. 2018. *Religious Revitalization among the Kiowas: The Ghost Dance, Peyote, and Christianity*. Lincoln: University of Nebraska Press.

LaBarre, R. Weston. 1957. *Autobiography of a Kiowa Indian*. Madison WI: Microcard Foundation.

Lassiter, Luke Eric. 2005. "Kiowa Indian Hymns." In *American Indian Religious Traditions: An Encyclopedia*, edited by Suzanne J. Crawford and Dennis F. Kelley, 440–42. Santa Barbara CA: ABC-CLIO.

Lee, Robert E. 1993. "It's a Bird, It's a Plane, No, It's . . ." *Oklahoman*, May 31, 1993. https://oklahoman.com/article/2432144/its-a-bird-its-a-plane-no-its.

Linderman, Frank Bird. 1932. *Red Mother: The Life Story of Pretty-Shield, Medicine-Woman of the Crows*. Rahway NJ: Day.

Lynn-Sherow, Bonnie. 2004. *Red Earth. Race and Agriculture in Oklahoma Territory*. Lawrence: University Press of Kansas.

"Mapping the Second Ku Klux Klan, 1915–1940." Virginia Commonwealth University. Accessed May 27, 2020. https://labs.library.vcu.edu/klan/.

Maroukis, Thomas C. 2010. *The Peyote Road: Religious Freedom and the Native American Church*. Norman: University of Oklahoma Press.

Marriott, Alice. 1945. *The Ten Grandmothers: Epic of the Kiowas*. Norman: University of Oklahoma Press.

Momaday, N. Scott. 1969. *The Way to Rainy Mountain*. Albuquerque: University of New Mexico Press.

——. 1976. *The Names: A Memoir*. Tucson: University of Arizona Press.

Mooney, James. 1898. *Calendar History of the Kiowa Indians*. In *17th Annual Report of the Bureau of American Ethnology [for] 1895–'96*, pt. 1, 129–468. Washington DC: Smithsonian Institution Press.

Ortman, Scott G., and Lynda D. McNeil. 2017. "The Kiowa Odyssey: Evidence of Historical Relationships among Pueblo, Fremont, and Northwest Plains Peoples." *Plains Anthropologist* 63 (1): 1–23.

Palmer, Gus, Jr. 2003. *Telling Stories the Kiowa Way*. Tucson: University of Arizona Press.

Prucha, Francis Paul. 1984. *The Great Father: The United States Government and the American Indians*. 2 vols. Lincoln: University of Nebraska Press.

Tamez, Margo. 2016. "Necropolitics, Carlisle Indian School, and Ndé Memory." In *Carlisle Indian Industrial School: Indigenous Histories, Memories, and*

*Reclamations*, edited by Jacqueline Fear-Segal and Susan D. Rose, 233–57. Lincoln: University of Nebraska Press.

Teuton, Christopher B. 2010. *Deep Waters: The Textual Continuum in American Indian Literature*. Lincoln: University of Nebraska Press.

Whiteley, Marilyn Färdig. 2015. *The Life of Isabel Crawford: More Than I Asked For*. Eugene OR: Pickwick.

"Wichita Mountains." U.S. Fish and Wildlife Service. Accessed July 9, 2018. www.fws.gov/refuge/Wichita_Mountains/habitat/geology.html.

Woodson, Evan. 2015. "Strange Fruit on the Southern Plains: Racial Violence, Lynching and African Americans in Oklahoma, 1830–1930." Master's thesis, Oklahoma State University.

Wycoff, Lydia L. 2004. "Kiowa Six." In *Encyclopedia of the Great Plains*, edited by David J. Wishart, 124. Lincoln: University of Nebraska Press.

# INDEX

*Page numbers in italics indicate illustrations.*

# IN THE AMERICAN INDIAN LIVES SERIES

*Rights Remembered: A Salish Grandmother Speaks on American Indian History and the Future*
By Pauline R. Hillaire
Edited by Gregory P. Fields

*Essie's Story: The Life and Legacy of a Shoshone Teacher*
By Esther Burnett Horne and Sally McBeth

*Song of Rita Joe: Autobiography of a Mi'kmaq Poet*
By Rita Joe

*Viet Cong at Wounded Knee: The Trail of a Blackfeet Activist*
By Woody Kipp

*Catch Colt*
By Sidner J. Larson

*Alanis Obomsawin: The Vision of a Native Filmmaker*
By Randolph Lewis

*Alex Posey: Creek Poet, Journalist, and Humorist*
By Daniel F. Littlefield Jr.

*The Turtle's Beating Heart: One Family's Story of Lenape Survival*
By Denise Low

*First to Fight*
By Henry Mihesuah
Edited by Devon Abbott Mihesuah

*Mourning Dove: A Salishan Autobiography*
Edited by Jay Miller

*I'll Go and Do More: Annie Dodge Wauneka, Navajo Leader and Activist*
By Carolyn Niethammer

*Tales of the Old Indian Territory and Essays on the Indian Condition*
By John Milton Oskison
Edited by Lionel Larré

*Elias Cornelius Boudinot: A Life on the Cherokee Border*
By James W. Parins

*John Rollin Ridge: His Life and Works*
By James W. Parins

*Singing an Indian Song: A Biography of D'Arcy McNickle*
By Dorothy R. Parker

*Crashing Thunder: The Autobiography of an American Indian*
Edited by Paul Radin

*Turtle Lung Woman's Granddaughter*
By Delphine Red Shirt and Lone Woman

*Telling a Good One: The Process of a Native American Collaborative Biography*
By Theodore Rios and Kathleen Mullen Sands

*Out of the Crazywoods*
By Cheryl Savageau

*William W. Warren: The
Life, Letters, and Times
of an Ojibwe Leader*
By Theresa M. Schenck

*Sacred Feathers: The Reverend
Peter Jones (Kahkewaquonaby)
and the Mississauga Indians*
By Donald B. Smith

*Grandmother's Grandchild:
My Crow Indian Life*
By Alma Hogan Snell
Edited by Becky Matthews
Foreword by Peter Nabokov

*No One Ever Asked Me: The
World War II Memoirs of an
Omaha Indian Soldier*
By Hollis D. Stabler
Edited by Victoria Smith

*Blue Jacket: Warrior
of the Shawnees*
By John Sugden

*Muscogee Daughter: My Sojourn
to the Miss America Pageant*
By Susan Supernaw
Foreword by Geary Hobson

*I Tell You Now: Autobiographical
Essays by Native American Writers*
Edited by Brian Swann
and Arnold Krupat

*Stories from Saddle Mountain:
Autobiographies of a Kiowa Family*
By Henrietta Tongkeamha
and Raymond Tongkeamha
Edited by Benjamin R. Kracht
With Lisa LaBrada

*Postindian Conversations*
By Gerald Vizenor and
A. Robert Lee

*Chainbreaker: The
Revolutionary War Memoirs
of Governor Blacksnake*
As told to Benjamin Williams
Edited by Thomas S. Abler

*Standing in the Light: A
Lakota Way of Seeing*
By Severt Young Bear
and R. D. Theisz

*Sarah Winnemucca*
By Sally Zanjani

To order or obtain more information on these or other University
of Nebraska Press titles, visit nebraskapress.unl.edu.